# THE KITCHEN BIBLE

Designing the perfect culinary space

Barbara Ballinger and Margaret Crane with designer Jennifer Gilmer

# THE KITCHEN BIBLE
## Designing the perfect culinary space

images
Publishing

First reprinted 2016
The Images Publishing Group Reference Number: 1192

First published in Australia in 2014 by
The Images Publishing Group Pty Ltd
ABN 89 059 734 431
6 Bastow Place, Mulgrave, Victoria 3170, Australia
Tel: +61 3 9561 5544  Fax: +61 3 9561 4860
books@imagespublishing.com
www.imagespublishing.com

National Library of Australia Cataloguing-in-Publication entry

| | |
|---|---|
| Author: | Ballinger, Barbara, author. |
| Title: | The Kitchen Bible : Designing the perfect culinary space / by Barbara Ballinger, Margaret Crane and Jennifer Gilmer. |
| ISBN: | 978 1 86470 551 5 (hardback) |
| Subjects: | Kitchens—Design. |
| | Kitchens—Remodeling. |
| Other Authors/Contributors: | Crane, Margaret, author. |
| | Gilmer, Jennifer, author. |
| | Casey, Patrice, contributor. |
| Dewey Number: | 747.797 |

Edited by Mandy Herbet and Bethany Patch
Designed by Ryan Marshall

Cover: Transitional kitchen by Jennifer Gilmer Kitchens & Bath and Barnes Vanze Architects,
photography by Bob Narod.

IMAGES has included on its website a page for special notices in relation to this and our other
publications. Please visit www.imagespublishing.com.

# Contents

# Foreword

Our kitchens—the heart and hub of our homes today—have become a true reflection of how we live: a perfect fusion of family, friends, and food. We love to be around those whose company we enjoy—entertain and interact with them and often food is a major player in the equation. Today's cook doesn't want to be socially isolated in the kitchen while preparing a meal and this has led to different kitchen design trends emerging all the time.

At the same time, other trends become passé, though there's always the possibility they may return, usually a bit differently. For now, more homeowners want cleaner and less traditional detailing in their cabinetry. Transitional is still popular but not overly ornate. Cabinets can be dressed up with hardware rather than lots of millwork. Dark finishes on cabinets are no longer as popular as people use more white, beige, and gray cabinets with contrasting dark floors.

Because design trends change as much as fashion, though typically more slowly, and often because of fast-moving technology, I advise homeowners to think long and hard about how they use their kitchen and what they want to achieve as they start their remodeling or building planning. I suggest analyzing how they cook, how their family operates for meal time and entertaining, and that they leave themselves open to new ideas, which they can readily find by studying websites, magazine articles, and books like *The Kitchen Bible*. How you end up designing your kitchen is not just about getting a great return on your investment but also gaining a big return on enjoyment.

This book offers a total immersive design experience—from how to read a floor plan or a blueprint to picking the right design pros and thinking about kitchens of today versus those likely to emerge in the future. A resource like this arms you with lots of detailed information, so as you go through the process you can ask and get answers to all the essential questions. Many homeowners don't know they can buy two wall ovens and put one in one location and one in another so multiple cooks can work at the same time without bumping into one another; they also may not know they can raise a dishwasher to a more ergonomic height for their height; or that islands can serve so many multiple functions—prepping, eating, serving, paying bills, doing homework, hanging out to read the paper, or working on a crossword puzzle. But to achieve all those needs, the height has to be right, the material has to be practical, lighting has to be good, stools or chairs have to be comfortable, and the look has to please as well!

I love kitchens and, after more than 26 years of working in the kitchen design industry, I still find it exciting as I scan a resource like *The Kitchen Bible* for good ideas, new materials, equipment, and technology. I smile every time I get to design a new room for homeowners that can improve their lives many times a day and for years to come. I smile even more when they come back to me after they've used the space and are happier. That's what this book will help you do, too.

**John A. Petrie**, CMKBD, 2014 President of
the National Kitchen and Bath Association,
and owner of MH Custom Cabinetry,
Mechanicsburg, Pennsylvania

# Introduction

Barbara Ballinger  |  Margaret Crane  |  Jennifer Gilmer

Once a gleaming utilitarian room, today's kitchen has morphed into the heart of the home—a place to cook, gather, and entertain. While kitchens in condos and some houses may still be limited in square footage and more challenging to arrange, even a tiny galley-style space can participate in this trend when opened to a living, dining, or family area for camaraderie, conversation, and functionality. In bigger kitchens, zones are often delineated to organize different cooking and clean-up functions, eating, entertaining, a place to pay bills, do homework, and store wine.

Almost anything goes these days. How a kitchen looks stylistically has become more diverse with no single look, material, or color most in vogue. Gone are the days of all dark or light wood kitchens or even the iconic New York City "Park Avenue" style aesthetic with white cabinets, marble countertops, stainless steel bin pulls, big hulking appliances, and black and white tiled floor. Kitchens today can express everything from an owner's personality to regional design styles. To do so, bold or bright colors might be used—despite real-estate agents discouraging the look since many believe that saturated colors may limit potential buyers when ready to sell. Think about making it energy efficient,

as well as incorporating elements of universal design, so that you can stay in place as you age, or if you experience accessibility issues. You're the one who is going to live in this space; with proper planning, you can enjoy it for a long time.

Heed one piece of advice along the way—do your homework. The costs involved in equipment, cabinetry, and labor to make a kitchen look chic and work well for years to come are on the rise. With the average cost of a mid-range kitchen remodel hovering close to $57,000 and an upscale one about $114,000, it's smart to make prudent choices. Learn about the latest appliances, materials, cabinetry, countertops, flooring, lighting, backsplashes, and more.

But with so many choices, where do you start? Make lists of what you love and don't love about your current kitchen, walk through friends' new and remodeled kitchens or kitchen showrooms, and ask dozens of questions about price, durability, and functionality. Take copious notes. Scour the web for resources and bookmark products and materials that appeal to you. Take screen shots when you see a layout or a fixture that you like and save them to share with your designer. Or sign up with a site that will let you "share" using the cloud. Some sites, like Pinterest or houzz.com, let you gather photos of elements that inspire you and can also serve as resources.

Then, of course, use this book as your right-hand guide to study the rooms and suggestions from many of the U.S.'s top designers and architects. Go one step further and research some of your favorite possibilities, price them out, put them all on your wish list, and then scale back if you must. Most of us have to pare down once the quotes come in. Those glass mosaic tiles or that wine cooler may suddenly become a pricey indulgence. You can justify a pizza oven if you love making pizza, but be aware of the hefty price of that piece of specialized equipment and the space it will take up for its probable infrequent use. A good pizza stone may allow you to use your regular oven and save valuable storage space.

Remember, most of all, that creating a new kitchen is really about improving the quality of your family life, more than turning out the finest beef bourguignon, mile-high chocolate soufflé, or pizza. You may have fantasized about rolling out pastry dough on white Carrera countertops surrounded by painted white wood cabinets, but is marble really practical? If you're going to rush in with a cleaning cloth every time a drop of red wine or acidic salad dressing spills, you're going to start hating it! There are many attractive, more durable, and manmade materials. You may be happier with some of these in the long run.

If you see some feature that you must have for your kitchen, love the look of a certain kitchen but think a different floor might work better for you, just flip through the book and check out other options. Showing you the numerous choices available so that you can choose exactly what you want is what this book is all about.

Writers Barbara and Margaret have remodeled a total of five kitchens and written about hundreds more and kitchen designer Jennifer Gilmer, Certified Kitchen Designer (CKD), of Jennifer Gilmer Kitchen and Bath Ltd. has transformed kitchens for more than 500 clients over her 30-plus years in this business. Enjoy the journey, avoid the horror stories that abound, and get the kitchen finished on time and on budget.

# Chapter 1

# PICK YOUR PROFESSIONAL
## STEPS TO FOLLOW AND QUESTIONS TO ASK

Selecting the right kitchen designer, architect, builder, or contractor is critical to a project overcoming the inevitable obstacles along the way, plus being completed correctly by the end, on budget, and within the agreed time frame. You may hire someone suggested by a friend, family member, or a professional you've read about in a shelter magazine, newspaper, or online.

Remodeling or building a kitchen from scratch is too daunting and expensive a task to take others' recommendations at face value. Do your homework. Check references. Go see their work. Study kitchen design websites, blogs, and apps on your smartphone to know what to look for. Check out videos on YouTube that show how the process slowly comes together. Also, be prepared with your ideas about how your kitchen should ultimately look and work.

All these steps will help you know what questions to ask before you sign on the dotted line and work begins. We've put together a few of what we've found are the most important questions to ask—they may not all apply to your job, but many will!

### 1 Experience

#### What is the role of a kitchen designer?

Designers are the technical and creative arm of any kitchen project. They see the big picture and offer designs and ideas that incorporate current and long-term trends, taking cues from your lifestyle, and helping to clarify, define, and prioritize needs versus wants. They'll guide you through the entire process and help you stay within your

budget. If the plan involves structural work such as adding on or opening up the kitchen by knocking out walls, you may need to have the contractor bring in a structural engineer but for many kitchen renovations, a kitchen designer should suffice.

#### How long has the designer been in business?

Whether a designer, architect, builder, or contractor does a job well requires a certain amount of experience as it enables the professional to fine tune the skills and tools needed to handle everyday issues, challenges, clients, and workload—which is why, if the professional you're considering is a start-up, think twice. While you might like their ideas, want to give them a break, and you also might have great chemistry, be aware that the start-up does not have as much experience, and it's always possible that the business might not make it.

The longer a company has been in business, the more time they've had to put systems of operation in place so each job runs smoothly. For example, Certified Kitchen Designer (CKD) Jennifer Gilmer has had her own kitchen design business for 19 years and was a partner in another business for four years before that. It took her a good five to

**Opposite:** In Jennifer Gilmer's showroom, dark veneered cabinetry on the right seems to float; a trough sink is good for an entertaining space. Wall ovens are set at a comfortable height side-by-side and are flanked by floor-to-ceiling pull-out pantries.

seven years to find the right support staff to help make the operation organized enough to take on multiple jobs, know how to overcome obstacles, and stay on top of what's happening in the industry.

### Ask for three references

Before making a selection, it's important to get at least three references. Each may offer a different set of experiences. Some might be more upfront while someone else may give a glowing reference and not address what went wrong. To get different perspectives, you might talk to someone who recently completed a project and someone who renovated a kitchen 10 years ago, so you can ask about follow-through. Were items taken care of right away or did the company take its time and charge you for a service person to replace just a hinge? It's important to learn everything you can about the professional you choose as your partner in building your dream kitchen.

### How many kitchens does the firm design in a typical month or year, and is a certain number important when choosing a pro?

The number of kitchens a designer works on in any given month or year shows an ability to work in a disciplined fashion, is organized, and has a good relationship with vendors. Good designers should be able to pay attention to your job, too, regardless of how busy they are.

So ask: If they are doing X number of kitchens a month, are they too busy to answer your questions? Will this affect their ability to handle your project? Do they have a good support staff as follow-up? Are they good at getting back to you, if you need attention—sometimes quickly?

**Top:** Choosing an experienced designer with a good track record of satisfied clients is essential to a successful kitchen renovation. Design: Jennifer Gilmer

## 2 Certification

### Are they certified and is that important?

Getting certification adds another dimension to any expert's skills and demonstrates professional pride. Designers want to stay on top of the trade, will continue to complete continuing education courses, and adhere to a certain set of standards and ethical practices. It also means they're dedicated to the profession and have been involved for a long time. The National Kitchen & Bath Association (NKBA) requires that a designer has to be in business full-time for at least seven years before qualifying to take the Certified Kitchen Designer (CKD) exam to become certified.

## 3 Awards

### Have they won any awards and from which organizations, and have they had their work published?

Winning awards and being published reveals that the professionals really care about their work and will make every project shine if it's going to be photographed, judged, and exposed to a wider audience. It also indicates dedication to a job well done. Some kitchen design professionals only want to sell cabinets. Those who win awards and are the focus of editorial articles are truly designers who are proud to display their work and will most likely do a good job for clients.

## 4 Insurance

### What type of insurance do they carry?

Most kitchen design firms carry liability and worker's compensation. But it's also important for the client to ask contractors if they are insured and what insurance they carry to protect themselves financially for this job and your entire investment in your home.

## 5 Initial Consultation

### Is there a charge for the initial consultation to get acquainted; what's discussed at that meeting?

A reputable, skilled kitchen designer should meet face-to-face with a client to outline the scope of the project and explain how the process works. Most initial consultations, which may last an hour or two, are complimentary because the designer and client need to determine if they're compatible and on the same page with ideas, vision, and budget. It's at this time that you can assess whether or not the designer is adept at not only listening to you, but also is able to respond well to your questions.

In the first meeting, it's important to make the clients feel secure. Gilmer asks the homeowners to bring in dimensions of the room or blueprints of the house. Sometimes they bring in a master list of what they want, as well as favorite photographs. She uses tracing paper to draw out the kitchen plan and to illustrate ideas, and they discuss how the kitchen is to be used—is it to be gutted, added onto, enlarged by knocking out or moving walls; do they need a space for two cooks which requires more food prep areas; is the kitchen strictly decorative; is it the family gathering place; do they keep kosher which can mean more cabinetry and doubles of some appliances?

They also discuss design—ultramodern or traditional, calming, glamorous, retro. She then works up a rough drawing, and gives a ballpark price of total cost. This enables clients to make up their minds if they want to move forward and pay a fee to get going, or do more research and find alternatives.

Showrooms should also display a wide variety of products at different price points, so visitors can get comfortable with the range available from which to choose. Design: Jennifer Gilmer

## 6 Showrooms

**Does the designer have a showroom and work with different vendors at various price points or just at one price level, and what is it? And if they do have a showroom, how often do they change it to incorporate new equipment, cabinets, countertops, and other materials?**

A showroom serves as the company's three-dimensional calling card. It's another gauge of the level of the company's professionalism, shows prospective clients what they are getting in terms of style and showcases skill level and dedication. When you walk into the showroom, you can touch things and get an idea of the quality of products you'll be purchasing. Ask how often the company changes its showroom—updating it every five to seven years indicates that the designer is committed to keeping up with the times and trends.

Kitchen designers, architects, builders, and contractors work with a large variety of product styles and finishes—from cabinets to countertops, tiles, and faucets to decorative hardware. Seeing the options in front of you inspires creativity and thought. The showroom should include different vendors at various price points. This is important because it ensures you that you aren't locked into choices that might be over budget. It gives you important alternatives, and the ability to go with high-end cabinets, for example, and less pricey appliances, or vice versa—crème de la crème appliances and stock or semi-custom cabinets.

## 7 Trends

**Do they go to industry shows to be up on the latest trends, materials, appliances, or lighting?**

Typically, trade shows will offer new options in cabinets, integrated lighting in cabinets, flooring, countertops in different stones, floors that look like marble but cost less, tiles that simulate wood, the newest ambient and task lighting, the latest, greatest, and greenest appliances, faucets, and more. Perusing the aisles and seeing what is out there helps the designer glean new ideas to stay up-to-date on industry trends and build a network of vendors. Not all designers attend trade shows, but they'll still keep up on trends through reading, talking to others in the industry, and through local resources.

## 8 Style

**What types of styles are they most comfortable working with—traditional, transitional, modern, green?**

Many design pros have a specialty, but a good designer can work in any style if given the right guidelines. Caveat: Typically, if the professionals mainly design in Europe, they may not be able to design a traditional American kitchen as easily and vice versa.

**Do you need to show them photos of kitchens you like or will they show you some to expand the repertoire?**

It's a cliché, but a picture is worth a thousand words. A good designer can spot common threads such as favorite colors, love of textures, dramatic lighting, whether traditional or modern. Pictures also show what you don't want, which is equally important. Gilmer has had clients show up with their laptops and iPads to demonstrate what they like such as the white beach house kitchen in the Diane Keaton and Jack Nicholson movie, *Something's Gotta Give*, or the kitchen where Meryl Streep fed Steve Martin a piece of rich chocolate cake in the movie, *It's Complicated*. Favorite movies and television shows are a great place to start and communicate!

If a designer comes highly recommended and you provide the right information, lots of pictures, and ask the right questions, there's a better chance you'll get what you want from the start. A professional designer is also able to read clients both by what they say and how they respond to suggestions. You may think they like or dislike something, but a good designer may be able to pick out something else that is better suited to your taste, budget, and space—perhaps a cabinet or piece of equipment that you may not know about.

## 9. Fees and Retainers

### Is there a minimum budget?

This is a very important question. Some designers won't touch a kitchen project unless the client is willing to spend a certain amount. The final price depends on the size of the space, the quality of materials and appliances, and how you plan to use the kitchen. Any reputable firm should be adept at value engineering a design if the ultimate design presented exceeds your budget.

Keep in mind that your choices determine the ultimate cost. Is it merely decorative? Are you really going to use it as a working kitchen, or just heat up a turkey from a supermarket for a holiday meal with everybody helping to bring the side dishes and desserts?

There are always materials that cost less—an attractive look-a-like man-made quartz from Caesarstone, Silestone, or Cambria among other manufacturers instead of pricey marble, for example. You may not have to have a six-burner professional style range for $4,000 to $15,000 where a four-burner priced from $1,500 to $3,000 can work well. Appearance is key when you make your cabinet selection and options include the door style (full overlay, partial overlay, or inset), wood species, stain, finish, paint color, and whether it will be framed or unframed. Interest is just as key, but if you want your cabinets to last a long time—20 to 40 years—you'll want to go with ones that are higher quality.

Other questions that may arise:

**How much of a retainer do they require to start a project and do they apply it toward the final cost?**

**How often will they charge you for work completed?**

**Are you able to hold back a portion until everything is completed to your satisfaction?**

Most designers will charge a non-refundable retainer fee that can vary widely from a nominal $500 to a percentage of the preliminary estimate. Some designers may charge an hourly fee as well. Reputable firms often require an additional deposit before releasing project drawings because preparing the floor plan and elevations require more work than the retainer covers. Depending on the firm's policy, this deposit may be credited toward your balance.

A talented firm will need an additional deposit to release the drawings because a project involves far more work than $3,000 worth, for example. Fees for kitchen designers are different from architects or interior designers. Kitchen designers only make their money when they sell materials to create a new kitchen. Once the cabinets are ordered—as well as other materials, your designer should set up a payment schedule for the remainder.

Holding back a portion until everything on the punch list is completed is not an option with the design as the materials are usually all custom-ordered for a project and must be paid for prior to delivery. This is the same as buying furniture, always COD; you'll need to pay when the materials are delivered. When choosing to hold back a portion of your payment, you may only hold back payment of the labor charges, not the fees for materials.

If you go through an architect, they will typically charge an hourly rate for design, drawing, and meeting times. Then, you'll have to meet with a kitchen designer, and another agreement will be drafted. Starting with an architect when there is no addition as part of your scope of work may cost you more money than necessary. Generally, kitchen designers don't charge a fee for the design, but get paid on commission for the cabinets and appliances.

## 10. Appliances and Materials

### What's the usual process to choose the look, products, materials, cabinets? Is there a specific order?

Once the design is set, you and your designer focus on cabinet choices, door/drawer styles, and finishes. Designers should choose materials to give you a look that conforms to what they think you want based on discussions, photos seen, and maybe other rooms in your house.

**Top left:** Turned furniture-style legs, decorative corbels under a cabinet, and an extra cubby and crown molding show a manufacturer's precision woodworking skill.
**Top right:** Glass cabinet doors on the wall units reveal finished interiors for easy access. **Bottom left:** Full-height doors disguise a dishwasher to the left of the sink and the trash bin on the right. Touch latches on the drawers under the cooktop eliminate the need for hardware. **Bottom right:** This book-matched veneer creates a unique range hood. Designs: Jennifer Gilmer

Designers such as Lauren Levant Bland of Jennifer Gilmer Kitchen and Bath bring together disparate materials to make a space as unique as their clients.

Cabinets set the scene, and everything else in a kitchen revolves around them. Since cabinets are also the most expensive part of your new kitchen and take the longest lead time, it's important to get them selected and ordered first.

The next step is to select other materials that are going to create the kitchen's entire composition. Make sure to get a sample of the cabinet door front finishes that you've selected and take it with you to the stone resource to select the slab for your countertops. Get samples there as well and go to the tile store next to select backsplash and floor choices. Gilmer recommends this order because there are only certain stones for countertops but many different tiles from which to choose. Being part of this process, along with your designer from the beginning, means you're less likely to change your mind down the track.

**Do the designers order everything that goes into the kitchen or do you, and if they do, what type of deposit is required for merchandise?**

**Do they provide discounts from retail prices on equipment, furnishings, and materials?**

Designers generally have more leverage with vendors with whom they've worked on a regular basis as far as price and lead times, and can better know what to expect. In addition, they have more clout if there is damage, back ordered stock, or a mistake when orders are delivered. Usually, any materials bought for the client would require a 50 percent deposit and balance upon delivery.

It is most important for kitchen designers to order you the cabinets because there is a lot of engineering, detail, and expertise needed to place the order correctly. The cabinets tie the entire kitchen together like the headline of a story and its lede.

If you purchase the appliances yourself, it's imperative that you show your designers the final purchase order from the appliance dealer so they can make sure all is correct and will fit. It can be risky to order on your own because once you've signed off at delivery, it's impossible to get an appliance replaced if it's the wrong one or if it is damaged. Bear in mind that there is very little mark-up on appliances, and often there really isn't much to save by shopping around.

Gilmer also encourages her clients to buy the countertops through her to make sure they fit correctly and that faucet holes are drilled in the proper positions. Her firm is then responsible for any problems and has the leverage to make sure if something goes awry that it will be fixed properly.

## 11 The Design

**How many design meetings will you typically have before the plan is finalized, and also how many revisions are permitted?**

Some designers design in their office with you, the client, right there, so they can incorporate your input. Gilmer designs a simple layout the first time that she meets you in order to facilitate discussion and creativity. In this meeting, she explains the mechanics of the kitchen with some preliminary thought to aesthetics, so that you can give meaningful, educated suggestions or make changes. All revisions are not a problem at this point.

There are several more meetings, each time with more and more detail, before the detailed final design is fleshed out, and it can take six weeks to three months of meetings, working on revisions, checking the plan again before anything is ordered.

When the detailed plan is completed, the drawings are very complex. If you request a major change in the layout and design at that point, additional fees may be discussed. This rarely happens because you've been kept in the loop through the whole process. The additional fee is in place to discourage you from making huge changes at this stage. It's a good idea to ask your designer upfront to clarify the policy regarding these changes.

## 12 Measurements

### When are measurements taken?

Gilmer makes decisions based on the project scope: If she's working solely with the existing kitchen, the space is measured as soon as her firm is retained. If there are going to be additions to the kitchen, she'll use the architect's plans for preliminary design purposes and then measure on-site once the rough studs are up. Because the lead time for cabinets varies between 8 and 12 weeks, it is critical to get measurements quickly. If it's a new house, she'll use the plans to design, then measure as soon as the kitchen area is framed, making allowances for drywall and wall finishes.

## 13 Architects, Designers, and Contractors

### If you're adding or gutting the entire space, what exactly will an architect or designer offer, or will a contractor suffice?

If you're taking out interior walls, typically the contractors can tell you if they are load-bearing walls that must be retained and if any beams need to be added to compensate. If they're not sure and/or if they are, they would ask a structural engineer to make a definite determination. This may cost an additional $600 to $2,000, depending on the room's complexity and the area of the country where work is done. There is no need to hire architects for this work, unless they are involved in the design as well.

A contractor doesn't do the design work, but rather handles the construction and hires sub-contractors to complete the job based on what the designer, builder, or architect drafts. Simply put, the designer manages the design and orders materials and then once the work starts, the contractor manages the job since they are on-site on a daily basis.

## 14 Hiring and Oversight

### Who officially hires the contractor and what questions should you ask?

Ideally, you would hire the contractor. If you choose someone the designer uses on a regular basis, again, it becomes an extension of their team. If you hire someone you know, the designer will still work as a team with that tradesperson, but there's a learning curve of working together.

Before hiring someone, try to see some of their work. Ask how many kitchens they work on a year. What types of cabinets do they install—custom, semi-custom, or stock? The contractors might not specialize in kitchens and you want someone who does. It doesn't make sense just to hire a contractor because you think he's a good carpenter—installing cabinets is a specialty and many contractors use finish carpenters who don't always have the same experience as real cabinet installers do. It takes a seasoned cabinet installer a good 5 to 10 years to be able to handle a complex, custom kitchen installation.

When hiring a contractor, listen to descriptions of their work, get references, go see some completed work, and always sign a separate contract. The most important elements are trust and reliability—this person will get to know you and how you live better than your best friend. Ask the same questions you would ask a potential designer.

## 15 Permits and Local Governance

### What hours will the contractors typically work—your neighborhood or building may have rules about hours and weekend noise; also, who looks after the building permits?

Contractors are all aware of this issue, so ask them directly. Most work from 7:30 am to 3:30 pm, but there are exceptions. Check with your building, neighborhood,

**Opposite:** Exquisite details can take a kitchen to the next level. In each of these four kitchens designed by Jennifer Gilmer Kitchen and Bath, a backsplash ties a kitchen together by blending colors of cabinetry and countertops. **Top left:** Aquas, tans and browns reflect the colors of the outdoors in this mosaic backsplash for a kitchen at the beach. **Top right:** Hot rolled steel panels disguise high-tech appliances under a weathered-wood-like tile backsplash. **Bottom right:** Polished granite countertops contrast with textured tile backsplash, laid in a diagonal pattern, above the cooktop. **Bottom left:** Slim, horizontal green and brown glass tiles add a spark of color to this contemporary kitchen with white and dark brown laminate cabinets.

or local authorities to see what hours tradespeople are allowed. Are they able to work on weekends and what time may they start? Many buildings don't allow weekend work because of the noise.

If you're adding exterior space to open up the kitchen and it involves knocking out exterior walls, you'll have to engage an architect to obtain permits. Architect's drawings are necessary as they will need to be stamped by both the architect and the structural engineer to start the permit process. Conversely, if you're adding a simple space, such as a small table area or bay window, the designer or

the contractor should be able to do the drawings well enough to get permits. It all depends on the design's complexity. Permits usually aren't necessary for interior work with the exception of a new electric panel or gas line.

## 16 Demolition

### When does demolition begin?

When demolition begins can be a sticky issue and another good reason to work with a firm that's been in business a long time. The installation schedule is

Replacing the existing wall with tall knee walls defines the dining space without separating it from the kitchen in this Jennifer Gilmer design. Enlarging the single door with mullioned French doors floods the new kitchen with light.

usually determined by the cabinet delivery date and demolition may begin up to a week before they arrive. This ensures that the contractors are ready for each stage of the renovation.

## 17 Sub-contractors and Staffing

**Does the designer have sub-contractors on staff or contract out all work—electrical, plumbing, and demolition—and, if the latter is the case, are these regular subs?**

**Do the sub-contractors carry their own insurance?**

The contractors Gilmer uses have subs they regularly work with and they set the schedule. They know what's expected from each tradesperson and in what order they need be at the job site. Each member is expected to show up on time and clean up daily. On occasion, this may not go exactly as planned because of previous jobs running late. In these cases, the contractor should be able to find solutions that keep the ball rolling.

When choosing a kitchen contractor, it's often best to work with a small company—parent and child or sole owner—rather than a huge business that has upper management and overhead, which can make the job more expensive. It doesn't make sense to use a big expensive firm to do a kitchen unless it's specialized in such work, or if the project is extensive and includes other rooms such as a butler's pantry, laundry, mud room, and perhaps a family room.

In the U.S., many states require that home improvement contractors show proof of insurance as part of the licensing process and these policies cover damage or injuries caused by the contractor and provide payments to injured workers. In the same way, many states also require home improvement contractors obtain a Surety Bond (amounts vary by state) to ensure that the project will be completed per the contract. Ideally, you should ask potential contractors to see their insurance and bond certificates and call the insurance companies to make sure that the policies are in effect.

## 18 Cleanliness

**Will the work area be cleaned daily or weekly with trash and old appliances and cabinets hauled away?**

It's a shame to throw away cabinets that still retain some life. In the past, they would just go to the dump or landfill, but now there are many companies that will take old cabinets and resell or donate them. Check in your area to see what companies will do this.

Because demolition will create a lot of dust that will float all over your house, be sure to ask how the contractors plan to seal off the kitchen when they're working. They should use heavy plastic with zippers that are firmly sealed around doors to make the best effort to contain dust and dirt. The area should be swept clean at the end of each day, especially if you're living in the home while work is done. In some cases, the contractor will order a rollaway trash container and place it in your street or driveway, or, he may simply haul away debris, trash, and old appliances on a regular basis.

## 19 Contact

**How will you stay in touch—by phone or email? How will you resolve differences if work or workers are unsatisfactory?**

Most contractors now use email. This is a good way to communicate since all communication is recorded, and it's quick and efficient. Experienced contractors and designers should always be available and return calls or reply to emails and texts within 24 hours, if not immediately.

It's important that your designer is your advocate. To resolve differences, keep your designer informed of any concerns. If it's a contractor problem, the designer may offer to talk to the contractor, if you'd prefer. Most often, it's best to meet in the home with all parties present to find a solution. A lot of times, complaints are related to the time frame of getting work done. Keep in mind that it's normal for a day or two to go by while waiting for a subcontractor to be able to get to the site, but if this happens frequently or for longer periods of time, it needs to be addressed.

Once the countertops have been delivered, the job should be completed within the next two to three weeks at most. All of this is another very good reason to select a contractor who is recommended by the designer because ultimately the designer can be a more effective advocate for you. The line of communication is more open and the contractors know what the designer expects.

## 20 Completion

**How long should you expect the total project to take? If it goes much longer, is there any reimbursement back to the client?**

You might be able to write language into the contract deducting or holding back a certain amount of the final contract payment for each day the contractor does not meet the deadline if the delay is the contractor's fault.

A project remodel should take six to eight weeks, which includes two weeks waiting time for the countertops. If the job is complicated—if you're gutting the downstairs and putting in new walls, replacing or adding windows or doors, taking down a load-bearing wall—the project could take an additional two to four weeks. Be prepared and add in extra time for installation delays, unseen damage that needs to be addressed, or hidden pipes that couldn't be seen before demolition. Have a place where you can do light cooking, such as a laundry or basement, since kitchens don't get remodeled or built overnight, and frustration can easily set in with nightly take-out and eating out. Your contractor should help set up a makeshift kitchen.

The good news is that when working with good designers with a smooth system, they know ahead of time what to do to avoid delays. In some cases,

they'll find an alternative that can be delivered quickly. Sometimes it's the homeowners who make changes and cause the delays, but even in these cases, a reputable firm will do its best to expedite these changes without too much inconvenience and extra expense.

## 21 Warranties

**How long are warranties good for cabinets, appliances, other materials, and workmanship?**

Warranties are connected to the company that makes a certain product. Typically, appliances and cabinets have a one- or two-year warranty, but higher-end materials will have longer warranties simply because they are better engineered and built to last longer.

They can be provided for whatever materials are selected, and your designer will help facilitate warranty issues that arise such as paint that starts to crack, especially within the first year. A kitchen design firm should stand by products it helped select for as long as homeowners are in their home.

If the issue is one of misuse—a finish wearing off because of scrubbing cabinets with an abrasive or alcohol based cleanser, for example—the designer can usually facilitate the repair for a fee. If it's a hinge breaking or something that is faulty with the product such as a joint crack that is larger than acceptable within industry standards, this should be taken care of free of charge. The designer would work with the manufacturer on issues like this, and it will send someone out to fix it or pay for a local touch-up person for the repair. For minor repairs, such as adjusting cabinet doors, the designer will usually take care of them at no charge. Warranties for workmanship must be worked out with the contractor. Typically, there is a year warranty, but some extensions can be built into contract negotiations at the front end.

# Building your team: Making expert choices

It takes a team to build your dream kitchen. Base whom you pick on their experience and their credentials. You'll never regret spending more time on your kitchen homework.

There's no single right person to hire as long as those you do are experienced and can offer recommendations for your needs. Your hires are your team, and it's imperative that you have a good feeling of comfort and professionalism since you're going to be working together for a long stretch—sometimes longer than you had hoped. You're also spending a lot of money—sometimes more than you also had hoped.

Following are key accreditations from leading associations in the US. Having certification can't guarantee success, but it can offer proof of greater experience in the field and classroom. Always ask about credentials and certification, but don't knock anyone off your team if they don't have it; you just may want to see more jobs they've completed and get more references.

- **LEED.** The certification is administered by the **Green Building Certification Institute** (GBCI) to reflect knowledge about green building and sustainability. LEED AP certification reflects advanced knowledge.

- **Architect, AIA. The American Institute of Architects** is the country's leading professional organization for experienced architects with chapters in states and cities across the country. Some architects also have attained LEED or LEED AP status, which indicates their knowledge of green building practices.

- **Kitchen Designer. The National Kitchen & Bath Association** offers a variety of accreditations, from Certified Kitchen & Bath Professional (CKBP) to Certified Kitchen Designer (CKD), and more.

- **Certified Remodeler.** This is a certification from **The National Association of the Remodeling Industry**, which offers nine specialties, from Master Certified Remodeler (MCR) to Certified Remodeler Project Manager (CRPM); a national directory of professional remodelers can be found on its website.

- **Certified Graduate Remodeler, CGR. The Remodelers' Council of the National Association of Home Builders** lists CGR contractors throughout the country online. These professionals have been trained in business practices that are helpful to the remodeling industry. An online directory on its website helps homeowners find competent remodelers in their area.

- **Interior Designer, ASID. The American Society of Interior Designers'** acronym distinguishes its ASID members who have taken time for training and coursework and passed exams from other designers or decorators, who may just have hung out a shingle. The group's NCIDQ certificate is another higher benchmark to indicate greater skill and coursework. The Association offers evidence of specialization such as AAHID, which comes from the American Academy of Healthcare Interior Designers.

- **Landscape Architect, ASLA. The American Society of Landscape Architects** is a national organization that trains and certifies architects to work in the outside environment and design sites for better aesthetics, functionality, conservation of nature and water, and energy efficiency. Some also design for special needs such as healing and meditation.

- **Landscape Designer.** Landscape designers are also highly trained to design a landscape. Their education training may be shorter than for architects but their on-site work and ability may be just what a homeowner needs. Check for experts in your area at **The Association of Professional Landscape Designers'** website.

# Chapter 2

# UNDERSTAND THE PROCESS
## 12 STEPS TO SUCCESS

Undertaking a renovation or building a new kitchen is a multilayered process, no different from following a successful recipe. Start with one that's been well tested; purchase the best ingredients, or materials; assemble a professional team; and carefully follow the method in the proper order. You went through many of these steps when choosing a professional in Chapter 1. Here designer Jennifer Gilmer talks more about how she and her colleagues move through the process thoughtfully and resolve all challenges.

### 1 Initial Consultation

This is more than a casual get-together. This meeting of minds is an opportunity to become acquainted and test if we can work well together throughout the entire process. We like for you to come to our showroom. Part of the reason is that I do my best work there when working with a plan view rather than standing in the homeowners' space waving my arms around in their kitchen. I am freer to come up with several sketches that show many ways to rearrange the space. In the showroom, I work on the design right in front of clients. This is a really fun meeting where ideas are thrown around, and I draw to see if they work. There's magic when you have a hand in the creation of your new kitchen, see how it evolved, and feel as if we came up with the best solution to all your functional and aesthetic needs together. Finally, from a pragmatic standpoint, I'm able to add up the linear footage for cabinets, countertops, list out the appliances, and estimate the labor for a complete rough estimate on the spot. Almost everyone wants that number as soon as possible.

Now that we have had this chance to get to know one another, you've had a taste for how well I listen and respond and a good idea of the costs involved to complete your new kitchen. At this point, you can decide if you want to go forward with us. The next step is to retain us for the design work by putting down a deposit.

### 2 Provide a Retainer

This is a good faith deposit that indicates you're serious about retaining our services. I would be leery of firms that charge small retainer fees because the retainer may be an indicator of how much detail and work the firm is going to put into a project. It also signals that the firm's designers are most interested in selling cabinetry rather than looking at the kitchen's whole composition.

It's very important to understand that this is a retainer for design work only and not a fee that buys you the designs. The designs can only be released after the cabinets have been purchased, or a substantial, non-refundable deposit is made. The reason for this

**Opposite:** An oiled soapstone countertop and sink, reminiscent of an antique dry sink, hark back to days gone by, as does the 8-inch (20 centimeters) high backsplash. A small space between the refrigerator and upper wall cabinetry provides a spot for versatile open shelves. Design: Jennifer Gilmer

**Warning:**

Avoid unrealistic expectations about what a budget permits. The first thing to ask yourself is how much will it cost. Before you come up with a dollar amount, decide what you can realistically afford. You may get off track at the get-go because you haven't done your homework or been through the process. In addition, you may rely on information from remodeling and reality-television decorating shows, which often are scripted or based on doing a lot of the work yourself, even though you may not be a professional plumber, carpenter, or electrician. When you go to a first meeting, don't just throw out a number like $40,000, which you haven't broken down into vital components—say, $15,000 for appliances, $15,000 for cabinetry, $10,000 for countertops—since the total already hits your desired limit, and doesn't include a floor, lights, hardware, labor, and much more. Also, don't say, "My neighbors got a kitchen for $40,000 and have everything they wanted," though, of course, you probably didn't compare what your neighbors got to what you want. Remember, quality and scope can be vastly different.

**Lesson:**

Make a list of everything you want and start filling in the numbers by talking to professionals. It's always best to allow 10 percent for overruns, which can be caused by unforeseen site conditions or more expensive material choices. Use that total as a starting point to know if you must ratchet up your budget or scale back your project's scope and choices.

is that a great deal of time and money is involved in designing, drafting, meeting, finding samples, printing out designs, revising and redrawing, incurring postage charges—all of which a small deposit of a few thousand dollars barely covers. Clients sometimes get confused about this because their architects or interior designers release their plans, however, they often charge hourly for their labor while we only get paid when we sell products—mainly cabinets.

### ③ Get your space measured

Most design pros will concur that, in order to be accurate, we have to measure the space ourselves, even if you have the original plans of the house, or plans of your existing space that were measured and drawn by an architect or contractor. Ultimately, we are responsible for everything fitting correctly and can't rely on anyone else to do this for us.

When we measure the kitchen for cabinets and other parts, we measure the entire space if the kitchen is open to a breakfast room or family room. It's critical that the designer take these connected spaces into account. We take a holistic approach to our work—the sign of a good designer—to make sure there is enough room for the kitchen table or for the family room furniture.

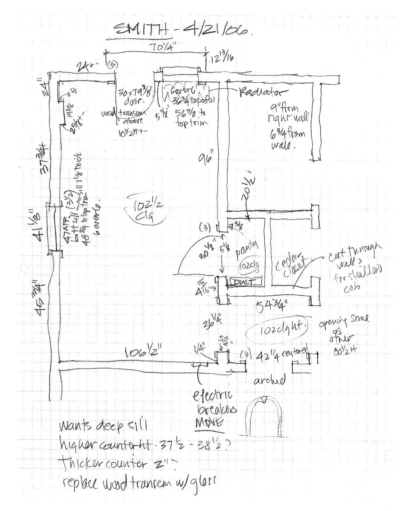

**Opposite:** An angled pantry offers copius storage and eases entry into the kitchen. The paneled refrigerator integrates nicely with the cabinetry. Open shelves above the fridge and to the right allow for display space, wine storage and easy access to cookbooks. The eat-in butcher block table on the left faces a nook with a charging station, television, open storage and a glass-fronted wall cabinet.
**Above:** Example of a "takeoff," the designer measures and draws this at the job site to start the design process. Design: Jennifer Gilmer

We also measure from point "A" and include the entire space all the way around. This process is very important, even though there are areas where cabinets will not be installed. It serves as an automatic double check so that when we lay the space out on our computers' AutoCAD system, we will also start and end at the same point in the room. If, when laying this out we find a discrepancy or spot an error in measurements, we will go back to find where the error occurred. If it's only off by an inch or so, this could indicate the walls aren't square and, in this case, it's not necessary to double check.

It is also important to measure the vertical distances such as the heights of the ceiling, windows from floor up, actual window widths, and doorways. If there is a radiator or vent that can't be moved, this also needs to be noted, measured, and included.

Door trims can vary, and some have a plinth at the base that is thicker. Some doors also have different trim at the top, which can interfere with cabinet installation and protrude past the trim on the sides. The aesthetics of the trim are also important to the kitchen design. In fact, paying attention to trim in the rest of the house is essential because in many cases, we want the new trim in the kitchen to either match or complement it.

While we measure, we may also have questions about what is possible to remove or change. Sometimes walls could be load bearing and may or may not be expensive to remove, or we might be concerned about how the hood can effectively duct out for good venting. In situations like these, we may ask our contractors to meet us at the house to assess the work before we get started with our design changes.

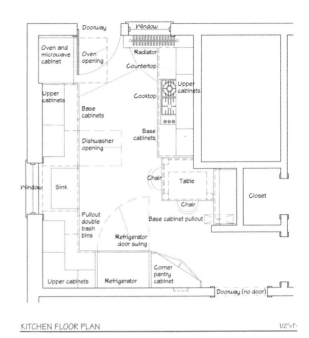

KITCHEN FLOOR PLAN      1/2"=1'-

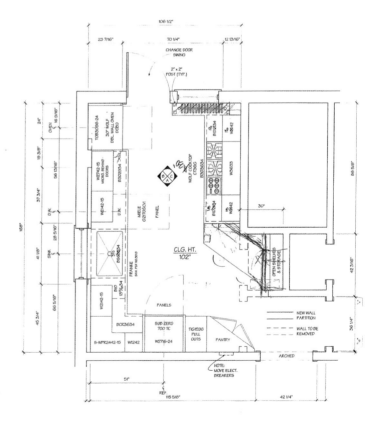

**Top:** Actual floor plan of the kitchen pictured throughout this chapter. **Bottom:** This is the same floor plan that shows how the designer played with ideas such as where to place the table. A dashed line indicates where walls for a shallow pantry were removed.

## 4. Reading a Floor Plan

Your introduction to your new kitchen starts with a floor plan or blueprint—a flat, two-dimensional view of your space. It is a bird's-eye view of the physical structure drawn to scale and depicts the placement of all doors, windows, walls, cabinets, plumbing fixtures, and appliances, with each item labeled to show placement and relationship to each other.

The floor plan will show wall and base cabinets, appliances, and where they are positioned in relation to a room's doorways and windows. Imagine yourself working in the space: Is there enough countertop space on either side of the sink to place dirty dishes? Is there enough room for a dish drying rack, if you wash some items by hand? Is there a convenient place near the refrigerator to put grocery bags as you unload them? Is there enough space to walk around the dishwasher when the front is down while you're loading or unloading it?

Typically, the sink is situated under a window to allow you to wash dishes with a view outside.

The dishwasher and garbage bins usually flank the sink on either side. If base cabinet storage is at a premium, some manufacturers have a sink base that can accommodate a roll-out bin in the sink base that still allows room for a garbage disposal.

There should be at least 24 inches (61 centimeters) of countertop space to the left and right of the cooktop, if possible, so you can easily transfer pots and pans. Ideally, there would be 42 to 46 inches (107 to 117 centimeters) between countertops, so two people can work in a kitchen without interference. Separating the cooktop and the oven sometimes allows for more than one person to be cooking at one time, so keep in mind how you plan to use your kitchen as you look at the floor plan.

Once you can "read" the plan, try to imagine yourself walking through the room and make note of what you see in each direction to ensure that it meets all your needs.

In this kitchen floor plan, we removed an existing shallow pantry door and short walls. This allowed space for a wood-topped eat-in table that doubles as extra preparation space when necessary. To the left of the refrigerator, we slipped in a corner cabinet to add extra storage. The wall oven and cooktop are separate so two cooks can work at the same time. Because the room wasn't large enough for a separate walk-in pantry, we installed a pull-out cabinet by the entrance where groceries and canned goods can be stashed.

Most designers and architects will use computer-aided design (CAD) software for the floor plans and will render elevations for each wall to help you further envision what your new space will look like. CAD software can also produce three-dimensional drawings that allow you to "walk through" the space to get a better feel for how it will look before demolition begins. It's always easier to make changes before the actual work begins.

## 5. Develop a Floor Plan and Elevation Drawings

This step-by-step process involves drafting plans and fine-tuning them until they totally satisfy a client. After dimensions have been taken, it's time to go back to the showroom and work on laying out the "as is" plans. We draft the room exactly as is and designate any walls that need removing with a dashed line. Typically, the floor plans are drawn very simply showing the cabinet layout and where appliances go. Occasionally, if I feel there are two strong possibilities for the new design, I'll have a couple of options to discuss with you.

Once these are prepared, we'll meet with you to explain what we drew and why. Many times, the design is very similar to what was discussed in our consultation meeting, but sometimes I'll think of options while working on drawings. This is the meeting where we really hone in on what layout works best for you and discuss the design in more depth. We also determine the appliances primarily based on style and size, with exact model numbers selected at a later date. This meeting will often last one or two hours. Any longer and everyone's attention starts to wander.

We take our notes and make the various revisions and additions to the design based on our meeting. Since we're getting close to the final layout, we'll also draw simple elevations of each wall, showing the walls as if you're standing in front of them. We'll incorporate most of the simple details—just enough to use this as a tool for our next meeting.

At the next meeting, I'll remind you upfront that the plan view and elevations are still preliminary. You'll see what I have while I explain that we'll be adding the details together. Most clients LOVE this part, but a small percentage don't want to be so involved. I have to gauge this with my clients and know when I need to fill in the details ahead of time. This exercise entails discussing the plan view again, with more details filled in at this point and then laying tracing paper over elevations. I draw in the door details, perhaps take out a wall cabinet and replace it with floating shelves, design the shape of the legs for the island, design the style of the hood, and more. At the end of this meeting, the drawings are more complete and clients are usually thrilled to have seen their kitchen come to life right in front of their eyes—and with their input.

We then incorporate these ideas into the AutoCAD plans and refine, recheck dimensions for preciseness, and fully detail them, so we can complete pricing of the cabinets.

## 6 Bid Out the Job

Once the plans are sufficiently complete for contractors to get a clear sense of what the work will entail, we set up a time to meet at the house to go over all details. We'll discuss if any walls are coming out and/or if walls need to be built, we'll point out where the appliances may or may not be moving, and we'll talk about the flooring and replacement windows and/or doors along with any other pertinent information.

The contractors also need to know about lighting and how this will be updated, so we can pencil out the plan, which will be formalized using AutoCAD before the job starts.

The contractors take notes and will bid out the job in about a week or two, depending on their schedule. They may sometimes want to bring a subcontractor to the home site if the contractor needs a sub's expertise to see something to verify that his quotation is accurate. But it is very important that the contractor bids the job and covers its entire scope. This also holds true if you work with an architect.

## 7 Make Additional Changes

On occasion during this meeting at the house with the contractor, we may find there are some obstacles that we need to go back and rework into the design. For instance, we may discover that we can't widen a window as much as we'd like to or that the load-bearing wall that's coming out needs to have a post to support the new beam. Usually, the remedy isn't that difficult and revisions can be made quite easily. However, sometimes the changes may be more complex and may mean we'll have to redesign certain areas, such as an island if there's not enough aisle space all around. These changes are all included in the retainer fee because they were created by job-site conditions rather than your change of mind.

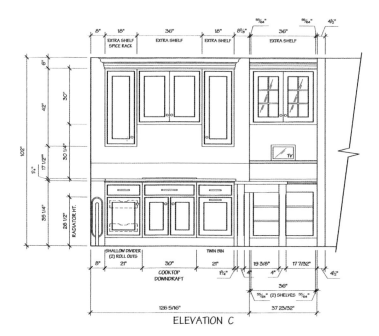

ELEVATION C

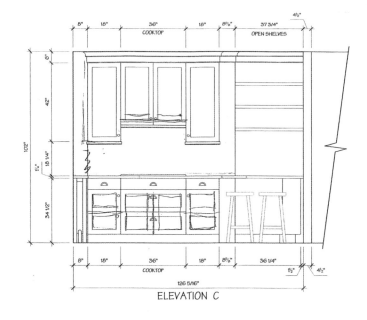

ELEVATION C

**Top left:** Extending the soapstone countertop over the radiator gives a little more space for prepping and easily holds a glass of wine for the chef. **Top center:** Taking out a small pantry yielded room for a butcher block table that extends into a charging station, media station and open shelves storage below. **Top right:** The final design approved by the client, with dotted lines in the far left base unit indicating interior roll-out trays and glass doors with mullions for the far right wall cabinet. **Bottom left:** Separating the cooktop from the ovens, now on the opposite wall, allows for a bank of wall cabinets where there were none previously. Additional storage below has pullout drawers for access to pots and pans. **Bottom right:** This shows the exploration of ideas during the design process in a hand sketch on top of CAD drawing to discuss the possibility of using stacked drawers on the base cabinets instead of the usual drawers and doors and open shelving instead of a wall cabinet on the right. Designs: Jennifer Gilmer

## 8 Finalize the Plan with a Contract

Pat yourself on the back. The design is complete. The cabinets and other materials are priced (or allowances given), and the contractors have submitted their bids. Now, it's time to get the project going and sign contracts. The contract for the cabinets, and usually the appliances is the first step. The appliances have to be decided upon at the same time as the cabinets for correct sizing of cutouts and front panels. It's also important to sign the installation contract in order to reserve the contractor's time. The lead-time for cabinets is typically eight weeks, but can be long as 12 weeks, depending on the cabinet line and where it's coming from. While waiting for the cabinets, I typically focus on selecting the rest of the materials, which have a much quicker lead-time.

## 9 Take a Field Trip to see Materials

All designers work differently. Some will refer you to a tile store and/or stone supplier and leave you on your own to put the details together. Some will select materials for you and present a few options for tile and countertops, which they pre-selected for you. So ask how your designer handles this.

I find that it's best to go with you to tile and stone stores so that you can see for yourselves all the options, and I can get your input. Walking into a stone and tile store with a plethora of options can be daunting. I always start by saying, "Let's just take a walk all the way through the store. Let me know when something appeals to you." Once we do this, it's much easier for me to guide you in the right direction.

I have the plans with me on these field trips, and once a few tiles are selected as possibilities, I will sketch in how they will be installed on backsplashes and sometimes the floor. Usually this will seal the deal between two options because tiles come in

certain sizes and shapes, some of which may work better than others. Also, the price may be the determining factor. We also make sure that the tile finish is appropriate for its use. Some floor tiles can be slippery and marble tiles will have to be honed, not polished, to help hide scratches. For the backsplash, we want to ensure that the tile is easily cleanable and doesn't conflict with the countertop pattern. The tile expert will have more knowledge about their products than your kitchen designer and will give advice on the various selections and how they will perform. Once the tile is confirmed, we look at grout samples to select one that either blends or contrasts with the tile. Blending it, most times, is the best choice.

If we have time, and if everyone is not too exhausted at this point, we can take a quick trip to a lighting store for the accent lighting: pendants, chandeliers, and sconces. If we don't have time, or if you just don't have the energy, I'll source lights online and send through my recommendations.

In the office, we gather all the information, figure out square footage, and get prices from our vendors. Another contract will then be generated to order everything for the appropriate delivery timeframe.

## 10 Develop Timelines for Work, Site Visits, and Payments

For materials, the deposit is 50 percent, and the balance is due for all materials prior to delivery. For installation, all contractors have a different payment schedule, but they usually require a 30 percent deposit. Then, payments are made regularly as progress continues. After we've designed and ordered materials and equipment, the contractors take over once work begins. They tell us when to schedule various deliveries, do the counter measure, and keep us apprised of progress or issues that may arise. Another payment may be due after the

**Opposite:** Cabinet doors and drawer fronts are "inset" into the face frames of these cabinets for a classic look that is further enhanced by the doors' exposed pulls and knobs. Design: Jennifer Gilmer.

demolition and the mechanicals are in; then, another after the countertops are installed. The last payment is due upon completion, except for a hold back of typically 10 percent when completion is finalised. Always have a final walk through with the contractor and designer before paying that final percent to be sure that all work is to your satisfaction.

During demolition and construction, patience is needed, and many homeowners like to have a small makeshift kitchen with toaster oven and coffee pot set up elsewhere in their home—a basement or laundry, for example. Once the base cabinets are set, it's time to measure for countertops. This means that one to two weeks of the timeline will be waiting for the countertops to be fabricated and installed.

The designer should stop by the house just after demolition and a day or two after the cabinets are delivered. During this meeting, the contractors will be able to get questions answered or the designer may want to point out unusual installation details. Most designers can't be at a job site daily, so they count on the contractor or homeowner to request a visit. If the plans are detailed and the contractors have worked with the designer before, job site visits can be minimized. Whether you are using your own contractor or one that was recommended, it's imperative to always contact the designer when it comes to any concerns or glitches to iron them out before unnecessarily alarming the client. This is key to a smooth, somewhat painless installation.

## (11) Avoid Red Flags

During the installation process, existing problems with the house may be uncovered. Be prepared, especially if you live in an older home. There can be termite damage, pin holes in plumbing, poor construction, electrical that needs to be upgraded

for the new appliances or more powerful lighting and computers, or simply poor prior work that needs to be brought up to code. If any repairs come up, it's critical for the contractors to prepare a change order based on the agreement for how much additional work will cost. These will add to the cost, but it's essential work so you can enjoy your new kitchen in the long term.

## (12) Tackle Change Orders

Change orders mean there's going to be a change that wasn't stipulated in the contract. You may have been warned by friends that change orders will increase costs—sometimes dramatically. Most likely, these friends did more than a kitchen remodel, perhaps an entire addition. For kitchen remodeling, there are rarely any change orders from the kitchen designer because all the materials are selected and prices set. There may be change orders that are precipitated by unseen issues such as those as previously mentioned, but typically, these aren't going to add huge expense. These change orders are money well spent to protect your house from further damage and so that it's up to code, which is also key when you go to sell it.

But if you change your mind—decide you want a small bar sink, or a second level on your island—those change orders can delay the project, as well as increase the cost. Try to avoid them or be prepared.

## Countdown

Now the room is ready to be papered or wallpapered in the areas where there's no tile. You're almost done and ready to undertake the unpacking, filling your new refrigerator and cabinets, and uncorking that long awaited bubbly. Bravo!

**Warning:**

Avoid unrealistic expectations about work getting done overnight. A typical gut job takes from 8 to 12 weeks from the time everything arrives and is on the site. Because of the time needed to plan the design, you should add in another month or so for that phase. Also understand that not all designers are created equal, even in the same showroom, so be sure you find out whether one is more skilled and more suitable for your planning, work time frame, and personality than another.

**Lesson:**

From the start, mentally add in a few weeks for unanticipated delays. Set up a makeshift kitchen in your basement or another room, and provide rewards along the way for your family to make the process smoother—a meal out at a favorite restaurant after the cabinets are installed.

**Above:** With the walls and ceiling stripped down to the studs, this space is ready for new insulation and drywall prior to the cabinet installation.

# Chapter 3

# TOP 12 DESIGN QUESTIONS

Good design doesn't happen in a vacuum. In order to get your job off on the right foot and moving forward in a timely fashion, it's crucial to ask the right design questions. Fortunately, you have a kitchen design professional to help you make choices and answer your questions before demolition begins, so you don't have to interrupt planning and installation.

### 1  What kind of recessed lights work best?

Incandescent lighting is on its way out and halogen lighting, though energy efficient, emits a lot of heat and requires constant bulb replacement. LED—light-emitting diode—lighting is the wave of the future.

The way these efficient lights work is that the movement of electrons through a semiconductor material causes tiny light sources to become illuminated. A small amount of heat is released backward, making these lights—if installed properly—cool to the touch. Because of the benefits of LED, insist that your contractors install these because inevitably, due to government regulations, you'll need to switch at a later stage. Many electricians aren't yet comfortable using these kinds of lights because the technology is fairly new and they claim they're more expensive. However, the costs are coming down. That's only at the front end however; in the long run, they are more cost effective since they last for a very long time.

When lights are for general illumination, they should be no larger than about 4 inches (10 centimeters) in diameter and, if they are going over a countertop or table, they should be sized down to roughly 2-inch (5 centimeters) fixtures. If you want LED lights to be on a dimmer, let your contractors know early on because it requires a special switch. It's a good idea to use lights that are directional when you want to wash a focal wall or focus on open shelves or artwork. Doing so can make a big difference in setting the kitchen off in a more dramatic, interesting way.

### 2  What kind of under-cabinet lights do you recommend?

LED lighting is a definite must for this application, too. LEDs are much more compact than other bulbs. "Puck" lights create a spotlight effect, but can be very hot, so much so that they will even heat up food in your cabinets. LED is not hot and is more consistent light that gives the best coverage for task lighting—cutting foods, for example.

**Opposite:** Designed by Lauren Levant Bland of Jennifer Glimer Kitchen and Bath, this kitchen deftly combines three types of cabinetry—white painted maple, hot rolled steel on the range wall and hood, and stained cherry on the island—creating a cohesive, harmonious space.

They are also designed to be less obtrusive. Jennifer Gilmer always recommends LEDs in strips that can be recessed into the bottom of the cabinet or a floating shelf for a flush application. They also can be dimmed, but you usually don't need to incur that additional expense.

### 3 Accent lighting is a place to show your personality, but how?

There are several possibilities: pendant lights, chandeliers, or sconces. These are all usually very reasonably priced, and you only need a few of them. This is somewhere you can splurge without too much cost, so be careful to pick one example that will elevate the aesthetics of your room to its best advantage! Let your contractors know that you want to be on-site when lights are installed, so they don't just hang them where they think the lights should go.

During the installation, it's important that the contractors hold up the fixture at the ceiling to determine which height works best for you, and for others who use the kitchen. Pendants should be hung fairly low, but not so low that they obstruct views across a table or island. A good rule of thumb is about 66 inches (1.7 meters) from the floor and not higher than 72 inches (1.83 meters). Chandeliers should be installed a bit higher, but not too high. It depends on the style of the fixture, but somewhere between 72 inches (1.83 meters) and 84 inches (2.1 meters) off the floor is good. When you see the fixture held up in place, you'll know what feels and looks right.

**Opposite:** The rear part of this room housed the home's old kitchen, which was gutted, enlarged, and made proportionate for the scale of the room by lowering the ceiling. Dark stained walnut cabinets are used with laminated glass panel doors on some of the uppermost wall cabinets for visual relief above a rectangular bay window. **Top:** The front of the house was bumped out to create a rectangular bay that contains the cooktop. Reduced-depth base units flank the full-depth cooktop and drawer cabinets and maximize the available counter space. A stacked glass tile backsplash gives the room modern flair. Designs: Jennifer Gilmer

### 4  Where should knobs and handles be installed?

Again, discuss this with the contractors for best placement and this is a time when it may be best to have your kitchen designer with you. Knobs on cabinet doors are often placed too low and, if anything, higher is better. The lowest point for a knob on a wall cabinet should be where the center panel begins or up just a couple of inches from this. For handles, it's safe to line the bottom of the handle up with where the center panel begins.

On drawers, the handles should be slightly up from the center on the top drawers, and then use that same distance for the other drawers below. For fully integrated dishwashers, ice machines, and wine coolers, don't make the mistake of thinking that you need a large handle. Just use the same hardware that is on all the other doors and drawers. For fully or semi-integrated refrigerators, be careful where the hardware is installed. Many times the contractors think the handle should be higher than it needs to be. A good rule of thumb is to start the bottom of the handle at about 36 inches (91 centimeters) from the floor; this way, the bottom of the handle is at about counter height, and it works well ergonomically.

**Above:** A paneled Sub-Zero refrigerator on the left is fully integrated into this small kitchen by Jennifer Gilmer showing great use of space with an 18-inch (46 centimeters) wide pantry on the right that pulls out for amazing storage. An open shelf above this massive 47-inch (119 centimeters) wide floor-to-ceiling unit provides display space and counteracts its bulk. **Opposite:** Decorative hardware is available in many different finishes and can add cheap chic to any kitchen—even inexpensive cabinetry can be enhanced with new knobs and pulls, a good place to splurge to update your kitchen with minimal hassle. Designs: Jennifer Gilmer

## 5 ) Where should faucets and other fixtures be placed?

The holes should be drilled on-site so you're there to confirm the most comfortable position. For some reason, some contractors or countertop installers think that 4 inches (10 centimeters) is enough space between fixtures, but this can be a big mistake. Typically, the faucet is centered. No matter the style of the sink, if the faucet has two levers on either side or one lever on one side, you'll want to space your disposal air switch or filtered water spout far enough away so you don't hit the handle every time you want to press it.

For most sink styles, you can go as far as 8 inches (20 centimeters) from the center of the faucet to other fixtures. If the sink is smaller, 6 inches (15 centimeters) will be fine. Pay attention to the side where these additional fixtures will be placed. If you're right-handed, you'll want the spout to be on the left, so you'll hold the glass in your left hand while you press the lever with your right hand. The disposal air switch should be on the right, so you don't have to pass your hand under or across the faucet every time you use it. The opposite would apply if you're left-handed.

**Opposite:** To highlight the beautiful curve of this solid stone sink, designer Jennifer Gilmer cut out the front of the Asian-influenced cherry cabinetry to fit it in, and complemented it with a patinaed copper countertop, a deep window box, and an antique style copper and brass faucet. **Top left:** A slender faucet becomes a sculptural element against a painted green glass backsplash and a combination of solid butcher block and Absolute Black honed granite countertops. **Top middle:** This thick concrete countertop has an under-mounted fireclay farmhouse sink, a filtered water tap on the right and a separate sprayer on the left. **Top right:** A separate pot filler faucet eliminates the need to carry heavy loads across the kitchen. Designs: Jennifer Gilmer

### 6 How high or low should a hood be placed?

Make sure the hood isn't installed too low or you'll hit your head. This is often the first complaint from a client about an existing kitchen. Appliance companies typically recommend the hood be 30 inches (76 centimeters) above the counter because the closer the hood is to the cooking surface, the more effective it will be. That's great, but not if you're going to constantly bump into it! If you do the math, this 30 inches (76 centimeters) plus the 36-inch (91 centimeters) height of the countertop puts the hood at 66 inches (1.7 meters). If you're taller than that, you'll hit your head every time you go near that area. Raising the hood to 33 to 36 inches (83 to 91 centimeters) off the cooking surface only minimally changes the hood's effectiveness, but allows you to be comfortable while standing and working.

**Opposite:** This old-world steel hood is surrounded by new cabinets manufactured to look like they've been painted many times. To add more period detail, Craftsman-style strap hinges and a hand-painted backsplash were used. **Left:** To accommodate a tall homeowner, this hood was hung a bit higher than the manufacturer's recommendation. The hood's effectiveness was compromised somewhat, but that was better for the owner while at the stove. **Right:** High ceilings accented with wood beams allowed room for a massive paneled hood with sumptuous moldings that is stepped back to allow for natural light from a window on the right. Oversized natural slate floor tiles tie together the granite countertops and ochre backsplash. Designs: Jennifer Gilmer

**7** **Should I install a single- or double-bowl sink, and also one large and a second, smaller sink if I have room?**

Most clients these days seem to prefer a large single bowl, typically 30 inches (76 centimeters) wide. I feel that one large bowl is preferred now because the days of washing and rinsing dishes are long gone. With oven racks, broiling pans, cookie sheets, and casserole dishes getting larger and larger, wider sinks make doing the dishes much easier. If you're concerned about wanting to be able to do two tasks at the same time—for example, having a place to put dirty dishes, but also be able to wash and peel veggies— you can always put a large bowl in the sink for the veggies. That way, there'll still be plenty of room for dirty dishes.

The front to back dimension has also been enlarged over the years. If it's 30 inches (76 centimeters) wide and only 16 inches (40 centimeters) from front to back, then it almost feels like a trough sink. Try to use a sink that is 18 inches (46 centimeters) front to back. Beware, however, with a thick backsplash and a windowsill, fitting the faucet in can be tricky. If this is the case, it's best to find a faucet with the lever on the top and not on the side.

If the kitchen is large enough to have both a clean-up and prep sink, this is a good idea, as long as the prep sink is placed closer to the range and not across the room. For prep sinks, we continue to use sinks that are 12 to 15-inches (30 to 38 centimeters) wide if space is an issue, but if we can, we prefer sinks to be 18 to 24-inches (46 to 61 centimeters) wide. This way the sink does double duty; it's not only a prep sink but, if an extra washing area is needed, pots and pans can also be cleaned.

**Opposite:** Two fire-clay undermounted sinks are featured in this kitchen—one a rectangular work sink that's 30 inches (76 centimeters) wide, 18 inches (46 centimeters) deep, and the other a 16-inch (41 centimeters) round prep sink that is closer to the range (not shown) for smaller tasks. Designs: Jennifer Gilmer

### 8. I have a bad back. What's the best type of flooring so it doesn't hurt excessively when I'm standing cooking and moving about?

Wood floors are always the best choice. They are much more pliable than tile, are reparable, and look great over time. Clients worry about the wear and tear mostly because many didn't care for them through the years. Wood floors can be polished every five to eight years. This does not require sanding, so no dust is created during this process. It's much less expensive to simply polish a wood floor than to replace the entire floor with new tile or a new vinyl sheet.

Vinyl, Marmoleum (an updated, non-toxic version of linoleum), and cork are also good options for those with bad backs. These all come in either sheets or tiles, depending on the look you seek. If you use vinyl, solid vinyl tiles are the most durable, but can be more costly than using solid wood.

### 9. What are the pros and cons of having a soffit?

Soffits are a kitchen design detail from the past and were used for several reasons. Contractors like them because it cuts down on the height of wall cabinets, which reduces the cabinet cost. They also give the sub-contractors somewhere to run mechanicals such as plumbing from a bathroom upstairs, electrical, or for ductwork/vents with less effort, and speed up the installation process. We remove soffits on a regular basis and while it often increases the installation cost because we may have to move pipes and ducts, the look is fresher.

We do retain them in some cases for some key reasons: they can offer a place to terminate beams in a ceiling detail; they can be used to cover a stairway that is impeding into the room; they can be used to hide transformers for LED or low-voltage lighting; or they can offer a place to install recessed lighting—although I don't typically like this because the lights usually create bright spots on the cabinets.

**Left:** In this kitchen, the soffit was structural and had to remain in place. Instead of enclosing it in drywall, a wood beam was installed to punctuate the soffit and add an interesting architectural element.
**Right:** Because of the room's extreme height, the designer introduced coffered ceilings with crown molding for more visual interest. Multiple-piece crown molding above the cabinets extended up to the ceiling required a soffit above the range hood. Designs: Jennifer Gilmer

**10** **Is there a limit to how many colors, textures, and patterns I use in the space? For example, does it help to have all the countertops and backsplashes be the same material rather than vary them?**

It's important to understand that your kitchen is a composition of colors and textures, all of which have to work together in the final picture. Clients often make the mistake of loving samples when viewed alone, without pairing them up with everything else going into the kitchen. If there is something you like which has a pattern, a countertop for instance, it's very important to select a backsplash that complements it. Too many patterns together distract the eye and make the room feel busy. Think of your kitchen like a painting. A masterpiece painting has one subject and everything else in that painting is designed to bring the eye to that subject.

For a sleek contemporary or minimal style kitchen, avoid patterns altogether. Solid colors and geometrical shapes should complement one another but bear in mind that too many colors can also be a mistake. What makes these kitchens so soothing and "spa like" is that they are fairly monochromatic.

For traditional or transitional kitchens, use a pattern in either the tile or the countertop, but not both! If the cabinets have a beautiful, exotic style wood or paint finish, make sure that all the other materials are simpler.

**Opposite:** Proper use of three colors provides a visual delight. White painted eye-level cabinets are combined with etched mirror glass front panels for wall units, base cabinets in walnut are complemented by a butcher block countertop in the same stain as the breakfast bar island and the shelves above it. **Top left:** Tile made out of stone was carved into a pattern of waves. **Top middle:** Add pizzazz with a Lumicor panel that's acrylic with embedded grass. **Top right:** Tile that looks like old painted wood creates a rustic backsplash for the hot-rolled steel panels on the base and hood on this cooking wall. Designs: Jennifer Gilmer

## 11   I hear such different advice regarding going with a range, or a cooktop and wall oven? What's best and what's overkill?

In higher-priced homes, it's a good idea to have two ovens in the kitchen these days. Double ovens can be pretty unsightly and rarely used to maximum advantage. A large, 36-inch (91 centimeters) range or a 36-inch (91 centimeters) cooktop with a 36-inch (91 centimeters) oven underneath may be a better option. For the second oven, use a smaller wall oven, which can be even as small as 24 inches (61 centimeters). Another recommendation is a combination oven/microwave, which can be used as one or the other or be used in combination for speedy cooking. It's also good for baking cookies or roasting meat, heats up quickly, and is more efficient for daily use.

If you really want a double oven, it can be placed inside a cabinet that has either retractable or bi-folding doors to cover it when not in use.

Above: The existing large Vulcan cooktop in this German-style kitchen by Jennifer Gilmer is framed by a custom paneled hood insert that spans the width of the cooktop with sides brought down to the countertop to recess it into a niche. Opposite left: Stacking three elements—wall oven, convection oven that doubles as a microwave, and warming drawer below—preserves precious counter space. Opposite right: What could have seemed like a massive wood element in this room has been cleverly designed with 24-inch (61 centimeters) deep cabinets, to accommodate an oven and a warming drawer, about two-thirds of the way up, topped with a countertop, then stepped back with 12-inch (30 centimeters) deep wall cabinets above. An open space in the center and glass doors on the uppermost cabinet doors reduce the bulk of the unit overall. Designs: Jennifer Gilmer

**Warning:**

Avoid too many imported or one-of-a-kind choices that may not arrive on time or arrive with problems. The light fixture from Italy you ordered got stuck in customs in New York, which means your timetable has to be changed.

**Lesson:**

Depending on the time frame needed, have back-up choices, and only order from the most seasoned companies, unless you're prepared for delays. Make sure that the contract you sign stipulates a way out. Cabinetry demands the longest lead-time—between 8 and 12 weeks—and is the decision you should make first because it affects the timeline for the entire project. Knowing when each component will arrive in advance, such as that light fixture from Italy that may take three months, will help to allay your anxiety.

**Warning:**

Avoid too many choices from small companies that might go out of business during construction or soon thereafter.

**Lesson:**

Always have a few back-up resources and know how well you emotionally can deal with delays. Check out the financial stability of any company you order from—if it's been in business a long time, there's less of a chance of problems and it will be better prepared to deal with any issues than a solo entrepreneur crafting hand-painted tiles or ceramic sinks. Manufacturers of home improvement products can suffer severely in bad economic times, so make sure the companies from which you purchase your products have a back-up choice in place.

### 12 When should I run cabinets to the ceiling and when is it best to have some empty space above?

There are a lot of factors that play into this. Usually, with sleek contemporary or minimal style kitchens, the cabinets should have an open space above. This is a very European look and was most likely originally driven by the way cabinets are hung there. There, hanging rails are used and they require space above. This helps the room feel roomier and more open. However, if your ceilings are very high, taking the cabinets all the way up to 10 feet (3 meters) can sometimes feel oppressive, making them difficult to reach, and out of proportion with the rest of the room and its furniture.

Many clients worry about having a space up above that collects dust, and if this is the case, then we take cabinets to the ceiling. If the ceiling is 8 feet (2.4 meters) high, it's best to get the most storage space by taking the cabinets to just shy of the ceiling and adding a crown or trim detail.

In many kitchens we design cabinetry to look like freestanding "furniture" pieces—usually a tall piece that's used as a pantry or display space. For this to be executed successfully, often we do not take these pieces to the ceiling even if all the other cabinets do. The logic behind this is that the furniture piece looks "found" and placed in the kitchen after it was completed. It's unlikely that a furniture piece can be bought to fit exactly the correct height and match other cabinets that go almost to the ceiling. And thank goodness in many cases, since they give a kitchen more visual variety and interest.

**Opposite top:** Omitting wall cabinets in this Belgian-style kitchen gives it a European flair, suggesting that the range hood hangs on a stone wall. To make up for lost storage capacity, an oversized floor-to-ceiling pantry is on the opposite side. **Opposite bottom:** To add enough storage, Gilmer installed a row of floor-to-ceiling cabinets. **Top:** These wall cabinets were installed leaving a reveal of about 5 inches (12 centimeters) of tiled wall space above them to give the illusion that the cabinets are hung on a fully tiled wall—a popular look in Europe. Designs: Jennifer Gilmer

# Chapter 4

# LOOKING TOWARD SAVING THE PLANET
## IN YOUR KITCHEN

We're in the midst of a sustainable revolution, and it's changing the way many homeowners design their kitchens. The challenge is to make them as environmentally correct as possible and still achieve the desired result within your budget.

Michelle Kolbe, COO and co-founder of EvoDOMUS, a green prefabrication company, works with many of the most important elements that go into sustainable kitchens to help her homeowner-clients who want to be environmentally aware, a trend that she's seen increase over recent years. She thinks doing so is prudent for the planet, homes, and individual healthfulness.

Before anybody takes the necessary steps, she advises homeowners to evaluate their priorities by asking these basic, generic questions:

- Is it healthier to do so, and how?

- What will I have to do to maintain sustainable materials and products?

- What about durability? Will the product/ products last, or will I have to replace them in 10 or 20 years?

- Can I afford them? Some green products cost a bit more, and some much more.

Good design and green can be part of the same process, though not everything green is equally green. There's a vast selection of stunning materials and appliances that are energy efficient and impact the environment—including indoor air quality—far less than non-sustainable products do. The following should be on the top of every list, according to Kolbe:

- Use green products and building materials made without formaldehyde-based glues, which do not emit harmful volatile organic compounds (zero-to-low VOCs);

- Save energy. Seal air leaks, add insulation in walls, ceiling and around water pipes, install double glazed/low-E windows, add high-efficiency kitchen appliances and light fixtures and use solar design where you can.

- Incorporate as many local sources as possible because it reduces transportation and fuel consumption costs.

Gradually, going green is becoming more the norm in new and remodeled kitchens, and some experts like Kolbe even think products and appliances that are green eventually won't have to be differentiated. Here's more to consider with specific suggestions, though the target is moving fast and changes are all about.

**Opposite:** To accommodate the owner's allergy-free needs, this kitchen designed by Jennifer Gilmer of Jennifer Gilmer Kitchen and Bath, used such green products for this LEED-qualifying house as bamboo flooring, cabinetry and 2.5-inch (6.3 centimeters) thick end-grain bamboo butcher block for the countertops, all finished with low-VOC finishes and paints.

## 1 Insulation

There are healthy alternatives to the common pink Fiberglass that don't cause skin or respiratory irritation or leak toxins into the environment, as is the case with rigid foam insulation. Two healthy types are cellulose, recycled paper that controls the moisture transferred from inside to outside and vice versa as well as significantly reduces airflow, and mineral wool, made from basalt rock and a natural product that is rigid enough to use under a flat or membrane roof.

## 2 Flooring and Cabinets

Wood is a great sustainable construction material. Pay attention to Forest Stewardship Council (FSC) certified lumber that guarantees the trees the wood is from were raised in a sustainable way, and don't come from a rainforest. The wood from this source may be used as solid, reclaimed (recycled), or engineered (prefabricated wood).

## 3 Cabinets

The cabinet fronts, as well as the interior boxes, are often constructed of particleboard, plywood, or fiberboard that is commonly made with fume-releasing formaldehyde binders or glue. Go for specifically formaldehyde-free and low-VOC alternatives that are available for FSC-certified plywood, particleboard, or bamboo. For a modern look, consider laminated or machine-applied high-gloss painted non-toxic MDF or particleboard, both of which use all parts of a tree. Additionally, toxin-free industrial-grade pine core particleboard is available and it contains no formaldehyde and exceeds all air quality and emission standards.

## 4 Floors

Cork, bamboo, tile, and reclaimed or repurposed wood floors are all great choices—the harder the wood, the better. It won't dent and will look better for a longer time. Kolbe likes FSC walnut and pecan, which are exceptionally hard and readily available in the US. If you choose an engineered floor, avoid VOCs in the adhesive in the floorboards and ridges, which are used to hold the different directional fibers together.

In addition, some prefer to leave wood flooring natural or wax it—this is particularly popular in Europe. Others want the finish to retain the hardness. If so, have it coated in the factory because by the time you bring the wood to the house and install it, it will have cured and all the toxins will have expended.

Bamboo, a fast-growing grass with low-VOC pressed into a solid timber, is extremely durable, hard, stable, and comes in many stains, tones, and colors. Because it's the fastest-growing plant in the world, bamboo is widely recognized as the ideal rapidly renewable resource. Some people, however, don't find it sufficiently durable for hard-working surface applications.

Cork is a renewable and low-emitting material, which means it doesn't leak toxic gasses. It's a recycled product made of recompressed cork granules and it creates a forgiving, comfortable floor. From harvest to installation, it is probably the most sustainable, non-toxic, and healthiest of all flooring surfaces. That said, we're yet to see a 10-year-old cork floor, so there's no information about longevity at this stage.

**Opposite:** Eco-friendly elements in this Jennifer Gilmer kitchen include bamboo floors, an end-grain bamboo butcher block, and durable honed black granite countertops. For the cabinetry, the sheet stock is PureBond, a formaldehyde-free hardwood, and the solid wood is domestic black walnut, finished with a custom-mixed stain that carries GREENGUARD certification for indoor air quality.

## 5  Wall Tiles and Backsplashes

What you put on your walls and backsplash areas can be very important if there are large expanses. You have several choices that are smart.

Porcelain tiles are one of the best ways to go both for walls and backsplashes. There's a huge selection of sustainable choices that are more durable than ceramic counterparts. All the large tile companies offer a variety of sizes and colors and are starting to list the percentage of recycled content. For example, you can get porcelain tiles that have 30 to 70 percent recycled content and some are even 100 percent recycled, in limited colors. Be aware, however, that these tiles often cost 10 to 15 percent more than their ceramic equivalents.

There are many companies that are particularly noteworthy both for their field and accent tile choices, such as Artistic Tile. Another, Iris US, has a large, well-marked selection of high-recycled content tiles, as well as one with anti-micro qualities that inhibit the growth of bacteria. A smooth, sleek tile, glass, or countertop material backsplash with as few joints as possible is a good choice as it minimizes grout, which can quickly discolor from dirt and cooking grease.

Glass is inherently "green" since many tiles are composed of recycled content. These days you can find a variety of shapes—from long and narrow to octagonal or simply the more traditional subway motif. You also can find glass in a full rainbow hue selection, and even translucent. Some companies use specks of metal—for example, Videpur Glass Mosaic tiles, which are made of 100 percent recycled glass and come in a wide selection of colors with prices in an affordable range, many now under $20 per square foot.

**Above:** The hood hovers over the rustic and coarse tightly stacked natural stone, which eliminates the need for grout, and provides contrast to the clean-lined stainless steel hood in this kitchen. **Opposite:** Gilmer uses back-painted glass in a warm orange hue to form an easy-to-clean backsplash and eliminate grout lines. Designs: Jennifer Gilmer

### 6 Appliances

Every major brand—Kenmore, GE, Whirlpool, to name a few—has EnergyStar® appliances in various price ranges. In particular, LG, Bosch, and Electrolux perform very well in the *Consumer Reports* ratings of price/performance. You can easily compare water and energy usage and gauge efficiency levels of those units in your price range.

### 7 Dishwashers

Spend money and get the best one you can. It will last longer and gives more options. The initial expense will pay off in energy and water savings and you won't have to replace it in 5 to 10 years. Also, consider how loud the cycles are. This is especially important for open-plan kitchens where there is no door to shut, and you don't want diners to hear the machine at work.

### 8 Refrigerators

One option is to buy the kind with water and ice dispensers on the outside of the door because every time you open the door cold air escapes. Alternatively, many brands now make models with a separate door for storing beverages and other frequently used items to avoid releasing too much cold air. EnergyStar® appliances must be 20 percent more efficient in energy and water usage than minimum standards, and you can save money on your electric bill. For busy kitchens and little, greasy hands, try print-resistant stainless steel or even faux-stainless finishes.

### 9 Ranges and Ovens

Consider induction. It's more energy efficient because it takes less time to heat and cook, you won't burn fingers in touching the outside of the pot or pan, and for many homes it's a must due to air-tightness and extremely high insulation levels. You will need new cooking utensils to make it work in tandem, however.

### 10 Ventilation Hoods

These can be pricey, but there are some very sleek designs from major appliance companies such as Siemens and Miele that look beautiful and pull fat and odors out of the air with circulation hoods and carbon filters. Fiber technology creates draught-free and uniform distribution of the ventilated air.

### 11 Countertops and Backsplashes

Many homeowners still favor buying a full stone or granite countertop. They start by going with a designer to a stone warehouse and selecting a big, chunk of old granite or marble, which, when cut to fit the room's dimensions, leaves behind a lot of waste.

There's one alternative that doesn't leave behind scraps—gorgeous countertops can be made from recycled glass or sustainable wood, paper, or ceramic material bound by environmentally friendly resins. The selections are vast and have clean lines. However, be vigilant and check out the best way to maintain the countertop you select. Does it require using a hazardous chemical product or will a dilution of white vinegar suffice? Does it need to be sealed and if so, how often?

### 12 Engineered Products

These manmade or engineered products use small chips of quartz or granite and mix them in a way that the end result is a durable, almost scratch-free, aesthetically pleasing hard surface with longevity that is great for the value of most kitchens. Cambria is a good choice because the company ethically mines the quartz used to create products that are non-porous and therefore require no periodic sealing. The selection includes more than 100 designs, it's family owned, and made in the USA. If there are local options available to you, use them, as that reduces the load on the environment in one fell swoop.

Manufactured in Spain, Silestone is also an engineered quartz product, offering a nice selection at various price points, and is coated with an antibacterial agent. It's a bit cheaper than Cambria, with a similar look and feel.

Made in the US, IceStone is exceptionally green. Because it's made of recycled glass and a type of concrete to hold it together, it does involve periodic maintenance. But it's visually striking and very sustainable; its downsides are that most homeowners don't want the worry of immediately wiping spills and recoating it every six months. After about six months, it gains a certain patina, which means that every piece is unique. It comes in a range of 20 colors and patterns.

Richlite is made by a company based in Tacoma, Washington, and is composed of compressed wood pulp that becomes a solid board. It's now offered in six or seven colors. It resembles Corian, but is warmer looking because it's wood based. Be aware that it does age as it lives in a home. Some clients embrace this effect, others don't.

**Top left:** Extra-thick end-grain bamboo creates the bar in this sustainable kitchen by Gilmer. The range hood is hidden behind the cabinet panels and supports a floating shelf above that bisects the pantry cabinet to the left. **Top center:** Here, Gilmer uses a natural slate stacked backsplash that requires no grout so it's easy to clean. **Top right:** In another Gilmer kitchen, 16 feet (4.8 meters) of glass doors wrap the corner and connect to the deck and backyard while a two level peninsula on the family room side allows homeowners to enjoy the view. The peninsula's elevated level blocks the view from the living room to the kitchen's working areas but, most importantly, provides a commodious and sculptural breakfast bar made of end grain bamboo butcher block that is cantilevered and repeated on the island.

### (13) Paint

Paint companies like Benjamin Moore, Kelly Moore, Safecoat Interior Paints, and Yolo Color House (in limited colors), to name a few, offer zero or ultra-low-VOC interior paints in all colors and are available at Big Box stores. No-VOC paints mean they have no volatile organic compounds in them. To use the term low-VOC, less than 50 grams per liter is required. No-VOC allows no more than 5 grams per liter. It's best is to look for paints that are labeled "non-toxic" and contain no extra solvents or additives. Many high-performance paints are available with ultra-low VOC content, but check the tints you may be adding for stronger color.

KEIM mineral paint, a German company, has a range of colors and produces it in an old-world way using minerals from the soil. The durable silicate paints and coatings last almost as long as oil-based paint without peeling, fading, or blistering.

### (14) Lighting

Lighting is key to sustainable kitchens and will become more important in kitchens of the future. Energy efficient LEDs have bulbs that provide warmer light with improved color renditions. Kolbe likes Cree, a company that is very active in design and offers energy-efficient, mercury-free LED lighting. She also recommends Philips for its AmbientLED bulbs.

### (15) Faucets

Faucets are an important way to slow down water use, and buying the best quality helps avoid leakage and water waste. The good news is that faucets today come in various sizes and shapes. Kolbe prefers ones from Hansgrohe, Kohler, or Kallista, which all have nice pull-down kitchen faucets. Grohe offers the Minta dual-spray pull-down with an integrated minimalist spray head.

### (16) Domestic Water Piping

Generally, polypropylene piping is very good, as is polyethylene and copper piping. All are healthy alternatives to PEX, CPVC, or copper with lead-solder joinery.

### (17) Disposal

Thoughtful disposal of your old appliances, materials, or even furnishings, is another way to be green and sustainable. You can resell them or donate them to a worthy cause such as a Habitat for Humanity or Goodwill, which can often refresh them for someone else's use. Some retailers offer appliance pick up and disposal services with the purchase and delivery of a new model. If you want to trash the items, contact your municipal department of public works to find out the environmentally correct procedures it approves.

# Amy's Additional Advice

Amy Gardner, an AIA LEED-AP architect with Gardner Mohr Architects LLC, offers more green suggestions:

## Efficiencies

If the kitchen is part of a newly constructed home, look for synergies between kitchen elements and infrastructure and other parts of a home to gain the benefits of heat recovery, plumbing efficiency, lighting, and more. To boost ventilation and lower heat—and costs, there are systems that preheat incoming air and save homeowners money while reducing carbon emissions. Also, for plumbing efficiency, use compact or central core plumbing. Keeping your plumbing areas in proximity to one another—laundry, kitchen, and bathrooms—reduces the time it takes for hot water to reach its different designations. When less time is spent waiting for hot water to get hot, your hot water heater is working more efficiently, less water is wasted, and it will lower your utility bills appreciably. Finally, depending on your climate zone, consider tankless or on-demand-type hot water heaters.

## Let There be Light

Consider opportunities for abundant daylight. Find the "sweet spot" between the need for wall space and opportunities for windows and glazed doors. Operable skylights with integral shades and insect screens are a great way to introduce daylight.

## Breath of Fresh Air

Seek opportunities for natural ventilation, preferably cross ventilation, in which air is introduced lower into the room through windows with screens, including clerestory designs and skylights.

## Keep it Close to Home

Consider designing the kitchen in such a way that is connected to a kitchen garden where you can grow your own food—fresh fruits, vegetables, and herbs such as basil, thyme, mint, and tomatoes for delicious and healthy meals. Or, design an "interior" kitchen garden for herbs at a window behind the sink. A great resource with tips on how to do this can be found at the National Gardening Association website.

## Regeneration

Consider a kitchen design that will encourage composting. Perhaps install a below counter composting system near the sink. Composting keeps organic kitchen scraps out of the trash and hence the landfill, turning garbage into useful soil enrichment. Save food scrap items such as vegetable and fruit waste, coffee grounds, tea bags, stale bread, grains, and general refrigerator spoilage. There are many good websites that give instructions on how to compost kitchen waste.

# Chapter 5

# AGING IN PLACE

Universal design in the kitchen used to be an afterthought. However, as people aged and started worrying about losing their independence and having to move out of their homes, common sense intervened, and enlarged doorways for wheelchair access or non-slip flooring materials became more common.

Today, universal design incorporated into the plan of your new kitchen should be the norm from the start, according to author, speaker, and consultant Louis Tenenbaum, a National Association of Home Builders (NAHB) Certified Aging in Place Specialist (CAPS). "It's what the name implies—design for all heights, ages, and abilities that offers a variety of uses and spaces to make life easier for any cook in the kitchen whether sitting or standing to roll out dough, chop veggies, look into the soup pot, or clean up after a large meal," he says.

To make your kitchens work to accommodate your entire family, here are some of his best design recommendations.

## 1 Counter Height

Variable counter heights are important to make reaching counters much easier for a person sitting in a wheelchair or a small child not tall enough to reach up. When deciding on the best height for everyone, pay attention to who's using the kitchen and how they're using it. For example, a range with wrought iron grates will raise an oven up 2 inches (5 centimeters). It's also best to vary countertop heights for different tasks. However, avoid placing higher countertops next to a range because that's not how you cook. You need a place where the equipment you're grabbing off the counter and putting into a pan is the same height as the range. Another way to achieve multiple heights is pull-out shelving and portable work surfaces such as breadboards and cutting boards.

## 2 Cabinet Height

Storage in a kitchen is prime real estate. To bring accessible cabinet storage to the countertop level for average-height people, utilize base cabinet drawers for everyday dish storage. Recognize seasons, and put Passover, Christmas, and other occasional use items in cabinets that are harder to reach. This frees the easily accessible spaces for everyday dishes and equipment. If memory loss is—or becomes—a problem, install glass fronts so you can immediately see what's inside.

## 3 Cabinet Pulls

D-shaped handles allow you to slip your hand into the pull and grip it without grasping a little knob that requires finger dexterity. Touch-latch systems also reduce the need for gripping and dexterity.

## 4) Turn Space and Doorway Openings

There are two issues you need to consider if designing spaces that may accommodate a wheelchair if it is ever needed. First, there needs to be sufficient maneuvering space to approach the door, and a 32-inch (81 centimeters) clear width to fit through it. Additionally, 18 to 24 inches (45 to 61 centimeters) of space is needed on the knob side of the door to grab the knob and swing the door open.

## 5) Surfaces

Solid countertops make good sense because they are easiest to clean. These include laminates, natural stones, and manmade materials like quartz. It's also worth considering heat-proof counter materials.

## 6) Flooring

Choose floor surfaces that reduce chances of slipping or tripping, whether wearing socks or shoes. Cork is very flexible and sustainable, as is rubber, in contrast to stone and tile, which are hard, increasing the chance of breakage or injury when people or things fall. Wood has great features but be aware that frequent cleaning can wear the protective surface.

## 7) Sinks

For easy reach, install a sink with a shallow rather than deep basin. To allow for knee room under the counter, it's best to have the drain at the rear of the sink and install the sink as close to the front edge of the counter as possible.

**Above:** Cabinet doors slide open rather than swing open. Sliding doors, such as Frontino from Häfele America Co., are a popular universal design feature because they allow users to open cabinets without having to maneuver around hinged doors that open into the workspace.

### ⑧ Handles

All faucets should have lever handles, which are easiest to turn. If reaching is a problem, one solution is to put the handle on the side of the sink, but doing so might interrupt your sink work zone. An alternative might be a foot pedal or electronic touch control. Use faucets with temperature controls to avoid scalding.

If you have knee space under the sink, combine safety and aesthetics by installing a removable panel over the pipes to insulate them from burning your knees.

### ⑨ Refrigerators

Shop for a side-by-side refrigerator with front mounted controls. Some refrigerators are difficult to open so test the doors to make sure they're not too heavy. But the width is a trade off. Freezers below allow you to reach frozen items and a good portion of fresh storage.

### ⑩ Dishwashers

Consider installing two dishwasher drawers mounted side by side or one on the left and one on the right, so you don't have to bend to reach the bottom rack. Some people raise the dishwasher but be careful with this approach as the counter top flow can be compromised.

### ⑪ Microwaves, Wall Ovens, and Cook Tops

Microwaves in the hood aren't a great idea. Rather, place microwave drawers below the counter, which are easier for all ages to reach, including adults, someone in a wheelchair, and young children. It helps to have all controls at the front of an appliance. Ovens should have a middle rack that's at or near countertop height. If you have double ovens, mount them side-by-side instead of stacked, or place the second oven in a different part of the kitchen. This allows you to reach the oven seated or standing so you can avoid lifting something heavy like a big brisket on the top shelf or bend down to baste a holiday turkey on the bottom shelf. Most ovens have fold-down doors, which means you have to reach over the hot door to take things out. An alternative is French doors or doors that open sideways.

**Above:** Drawer inserts from Häfele America Co. make it easier to see what's inside and reach items stored in lower cabinets.
**Opposite left:** LED-lighted pantry: Motion-sensored LED lights can be installed inside the pantry, cabinets and drawers. Adding lighting inside the cabinet, such as LOOX LED lighting from Häfele America Co., can play a huge role in both functionality and visual appeal in the kitchen. **Opposite top right:** Magic Corner II: Pull-out corner system in which just the front shelves slide out and rear shelves move forward. Keeping equipment and storage within reach using a system like the Magic Corner, makes a kitchen comfortable for all to use. **Opposite bottom right:** Le Mans: Pull-out corner system in which everything inside the cabinet slides out smoothly for easy viewing and handling. Häfele's corner systems and shelving features allow for easy access and flexible storage options.

# Multigenerational Living and Design

Multigenerational living, or three or more generations of the same family living under one roof or on the same property, is a cultural shift that will be happening in more homes in the future and will affect how kitchens are designed for all ages, generations, and special needs. Several factors are driving this trend:

- Elderly relatives who need supervision, and can either not afford to move into an independent living environment such as an assisted care facility, or choose to live with loved ones;

- Adult children who can not afford to move out on their own and can save money, perhaps to move into their own place, by living at home for a while;

- Single parents who prefer to have their own parents care for their children and/or take care of them if they cannot afford child care, whether at home or at a day-care center;

- Cultural tradition that preserves family roots—multigenerational living may sound new to Americans but is considered the norm in many cultures;

- A desire to live in a bigger house in a better area with better schools—with more family members living in a single home, they can afford this by pooling everyone's resources.

These reasons require a kitchen to be tailored to the needs of each generation. For example, some aging-in-place kitchen features, such as this kitchen designed by Matt White and Barbara Murphy of Neil Kelly Design, include deeper countertops to allow for wheelchair clearance, lower "upper" cabinets for an easier reach from a wheelchair, more accessible storage for food, hand appliances, "touch-type" faucets that are easier for arthritic wrists and hands to turn on and off, and under-cabinet LED lighting that provides good illumination when eyesight is fading. For younger members, the kitchen designer must consider their privacy, need for their own "space," and a built-in infrastructure (such as U-Sockets—standard electrical outlets sporting USB sockets) and zones for technology use.

**Top:** The former kitchen in this now multigenerational household was cut off from the rest of the house. Now a large open kitchen/family/dining room that is aesthetically pleasing, the kitchen features accommodations for every generation.

## 12 Lighting

This is very important both under and over the counter for tasks and mood. You can create a well-lit space using combinations of under cabinet or cabinet lighting, general lighting, task lighting, and decorative lighting. LED is preferred over incandescent and halogens because it's more efficient and long lasting. The bulbs won't have to be replaced for years. Dimmers on fixtures allow everyone to adjust the lighting themselves.

## 13 Light Switches and Electrical Outlets

Switches with large flat panels work best. Wall switches should not be more than 44 inches (1.1 meters) above the floor or even closer to doorknob height. It's good to have plugs and switches that do not require reaching all the way to the backsplash. The disposal and fan switches for the cook top should be in the apron for those who can't reach or might have sore shoulders. Outlets should be high enough to reduce bending.

## 14 Colors and Contrast

It's really important to start with contrast as a design feature of the space to enhance visibility. Contrast serves as a warning that the level of a floor ends, or you are at the edge of the countertop. For example, if you have a lighter tile counter, a dark oak edge or a solid material with a stripe near the end of the counter gives the user a good idea of where one surface ends and the next begins. On the backsplash, have switches or switch plate covers in different colors so that you can pick them out easily. A floor pattern can be an attractive feature. You don't want a beige floor and beige cabinets. Also, non-reflective floors such as wood may be a good idea. To reduce glare everywhere, use low-gloss finishes.

Most of us are pretty much the same size and shape. We are bipedal and, whether tall or short, can reach up to and down to most of the same shelves and storage.

Designing access for those with limited reach does not preclude all others from using it. Advances in medical science mean that more people roll and shuffle and live with limited reach, so following universal design works for a larger and growing audience or market. Changes occur not just as we age but throughout our lives. An accident at any age can mean accommodations may have to be made. Universal design is smart design with beautiful results that offers a special kind of insurance for enjoyment and use of your kitchen for years to come for everyone—family and friends. Your beautiful kitchen will work for you a long time whatever happens…or doesn't.

*A former carpenter and contractor, Louis Tenenbaum is now a leading thinker, speaker, and consultant on aging in place— the idea that our homes are the most desirable and economical place for housing and care. He has years of experience helping individual families, builders, developers, and communities set the stage for folks to remain safe and comfortable in their own homes.*

# Chapter 6

# THE KITCHEN OF THE FUTURE

The Jetsons' kitchen is coming to your home sooner than you think.

"Kitchens of the future will be stocked with appliances and equipment that are faster, greener, universally designed, more customized, and smarter—controlled from anywhere in the world by your phone or tablet," says kitchen designer Alan Zielinski, CKD, President and CEO of Better Kitchens, Inc.

As we continue to value our free time and are less task-oriented, we're turning to high-tech options to simplify our lives. One push of a button from your tablet or smartphone and you can turn your oven on or off, preheat, or adjust your planning while you're stuck in rush-hour traffic. More than 20 percent of Zielinski's clients incorporate these features into their kitchen designs today, and these numbers are expected to grow.

But kitchen designers like Zielinksi also know the future portends utilizing products in a variety of different ways such as placing a fireplace between two rooms and hitting one button to turn it on so users in either space can take advantage, clicking one button to turn off lights in a kitchen or your whole house to conserve energy, and selecting whether you want to heat your porcelain tile kitchen floor on those chilly winter mornings, but then turn it off at night when nobody uses the space. There are also motion and light sensors from manufacturers that go on before you enter your kitchen and off when you leave, a boon to the visually impaired.

A great example of this would be if you're watching the morning shows and the news hosts are talking about the best turkey recipe ever, you can now load the information on your smartphone or tablet, prepare the turkey, and link the information to your appliance to cook the bird. Oven sensors will automatically program the right temperature and cooking time based on weight and other measurements. All this is done almost seamlessly without having to open a cookbook or touch multiple controls. This same technology can also interface with smoke detectors, burglar alarms, and even the kitchen back door lock and garage.

Zielinski lists other components that will set apart kitchens of the future from those of the past—some of which are already available.

**Opposite:** In this design by Lauren Levant Bland of Jennifer Gilmer Kitchen and Bath, rustic beams conceal low-voltage lighting, which can be directed where needed. On the right, a wood paneled wall with floating shelves is topped with crown molding for a furniture-like appearance.

## 1 Open Sesame

Kitchens have evolved into the hub of a home, but the latest iteration doesn't just offer multiple functions but acts as part of one giant Great Room—what designer Sabine Schoenberg terms the Open Concept Kitchen, popular worldwide. "It broadens the kitchen into a family living space," says Schoeberg. For those without an open plan to start, designer Leslie Markman-Stern suggests knocking down walls.

## 2 Kitchen Command Center: Today's New Island or Peninsula

The kitchen island, and sometimes the peninsula, is becoming the command center and information source, particularly as many get wider and longer. Many of the high-tech functions in futuristic kitchens will be controlled from a selection panel on the island. Touch sensors will accomplish a variety of tasks from finding a recipe or menu that talks to you to pulling up a video of how to make your favorite gruyere soufflé and much more.

## 3 Lighting

LED lighting will abound whether to help someone see better to perform tasks or set a mood. There are cabinets with built-in lights that incorporate motion sensors to turn on and off when you open the door. Also LEDs will be used more under and above cabinets.

To make a kitchen technically savvy, LED lights need to be added, along with a dimmer system, which might add an additional 25 percent cost today. The savings in energy are on the back end when these bulbs almost never have to be replaced. But with costs coming down dramatically, many homeowners won't have to wait long to see returns on their investments.

## 4 Countertops

Instead of granite, which has become so ubiquitous, many countertops will be built from quartz finishes, according to the National Kitchen & Bath Association (NKBA). Although manmade and pricier than some granite, quartz appeals to many people because it requires less upkeep. What's very new is quartzite, which is natural, has granite's durability, and resembles more appealing stones, such as marble. One of the most futuristic materials for contemporary countertops is glass, often made from recycled materials and which can be lit for ambience by installing LEDs in different colors.

**Opposite:** A custom stainless steel range hood has decorative rivets and a powerful Zephyr exhaust system. Narrow pullout mini-pantries flank the stove and keep spices and oils handy. **Above:** Mother of Pearl quartzite countertops unify the white and dark wood cabinetry, sculpted limestone backsplash, and warm oak floors. Designs: Lauren Levant Bland of Jennifer Gilmer Kitchen and Bath

## ⑤ Ovens and Cooktops

Kitchens of the future will continue to have more than one oven in different sections to help multiple cooks work together—and those ovens will represent different types such as steam ovens, sometimes with a convection function, from companies like Thermador. In the future, the data needed to cook could be sent directly to your smartphone or tablet.

One new product from Whirlpool turns an oven into a refrigerator. Should you be late returning home, the oven converts into a temporary refrigerator once the food is cooked. When you're ready, it converts back to an oven to heat it up again. You will be able to program this process from your smartphone or tablet.

There are also ovens with devices that turn off a burner or preheat the stove. More homeowners will be likely to switch from gas and electric to induction for speedier, safer cooking, since a magnetic field doesn't transfer heat to the flat cooking surface, which helps avoid burns. For example, the Freedom Induction cooking panels from Thermador allow you to place a pan anywhere on the panel. And when your hands are full, self-closing oven doors will operate via a touch panel or sensor located in the toe kick.

If you have a smaller house or kitchen, additional equipment will serve multiple functions, such as Theramador's 48-inch (1.2 meters) Pro Grand range that offers seven different cooking options.

**Above left:** A sleek induction cooktop is flanked by appliance garages that extend to the countertop to minimize clutter in this kitchen designed by Lauren Levant Bland of Jennifer Gilmer Kitchen and Bath.**Above center:** Thermador's 36-inch Masterpiece® Series Freedom® Induction cooktop features 63 percent more usable surface area than most others. **Right top:** Thermador's 36-inch Masterpiece® Series Freedom® Induction cooktop offers the flexibility of cooking with up to 4 pots/pans/griddles in any combination, shape or size. **Right bottom:** The new Thermador range has a large oven plus smaller state of the art oven for healthy steam cooking.
**Opposite:** A combination of glass doors and walnut countertop make this organization/charging station look like a piece of furniture. Woven baskets inside cabinets hide clutter. Designs: Jennifer Gilmer

### 6 Ventilation

Hydronic technology is being used when water moves heat from where it's produced to where it's needed. This green technology conserves energy. Ventilation heat sensors also conserve energy and lower utility bills. A blower that's integrated into a make up air system comes on at an appropriate level to control the temperature and humidity, limits the return temperature, and controls hot water temperature too.

### 7 Electrical Outlets

The kitchen of the future will offer wireless "electricity," resulting in fewer cords. Almost everything will be powered automatically with magnetic sensing that operates on a magnetic field from a permanent magnet or electromagnet integrated in the sensor. Already the desk is becoming a dinosaur as fewer homeowners have big desktop computers; all they need for a workstation is a few outlets to recharge their tablets and phones. More outlets will be needed, but they will be invisible—built into the counters or ones that flip up and retract, or are hidden under cabinets, so they don't detract from the aesthetics of wall tiles or solid paint or paper.

### 8 Microwaves

Microwaves are more often being placed in drawers to avoid consuming upper wall and countertop space, making them more accessible for children and people in wheelchairs. They also offer visual and audio instructions with the help of beeps. Some microwaves are now being replaced with steam ovens for healthy eating.

**Above left:** A Thermador Freedom® Collection kitchen featuring wine preservation and fresh food and freezer columns also shows the Professional® Series convection warming drawer and built-in fully automatic coffee machine. **Above right:** The Thermador 18-inch (46 centimeters) built-in wine preservation column is part of the Thermador Freedom® Collection. **Opposite:** The Thermador Star-Sapphire™ dishwasher features a fast wash cycle, Star Speed™, as well as Time Remaining PowerBeam®, Sapphire Glow®, and more.

### 9  Refrigerators

Already, there is often more than one refrigerator and freezer unit in different locations in the kitchen, including in separate columns, as well as installed as drawers and beverage centers. This trend is expected to increase as more people gather to cook, work, and socialize in the kitchen. Water is also no longer on the door of many refrigerators, but located inside and accessible via separate openings to avoid opening the door all the time, which can waste energy. Some refrigerators will also offer systems that cool different foods at the right temperature needed for that product.

The future may also bring instant cooling, taking refrigeration and freezing to a new level, much like microwaves brought rapid heating technology to the kitchen in the early 1970s.

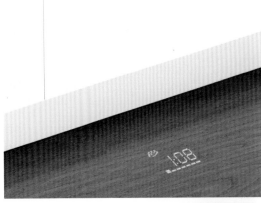

### 10  Storage

Running out of produce will no longer be a problem as it can now be monitored as you move products from one storage area to another. It will be tracked by a barcode-like system, accounted for, and assigned a place and position in the kitchen where it's best stored.

### 11  Dishwashers

New dishwasher models are geared more to saving water and energy. Models from Bosch have futuristic features, which include increasingly quiet technologies along with what can be called a "heads-down" display screen. This is the opposite of a heads-up display screen, as found in cars. The advantage to this system is that, without having to open the door, let the steam escape, and water drip on the floor, a little icon comes up on a LED screen in front of the dishwasher toe kick that is projected on to the floor and tells you when the wash cycle is complete.

### 12  Cabinets

Touch technology means drawers and doors can open with a button. If you're a baker and your hands are full of dough, this is a godsend as a way to open cabinets without having to use your hands and make a mess. Also, you might have cabinets set up as docking or charging stations for personal devices or smartphones that can be hidden behind panels that slide or open vertically.

### 13 Window Shades

Remote controlled shades, which can be operated with lithium batteries, will set the mood in more kitchens and reduce heat or air conditioning loss. They can be programmed with the date, latitude and longitude of the sun, and will operate automatically—similar to a controlled lawn sprinkler system.

### 14 Colors

This is always a personal decision, but trendcasters generally prefer soft colors—grays, whites and off whites, and creams—over bold colors to offer a sense of peace. This trend can already be seen in the most cutting-edge kitchens. Other colors will be used for punctuation—a pop of orange, yellow, green, or red—which also makes changing out the accents easier—and less expensive—when tastes evolve. Data on current color trends can be found online annually from multiple paint sources and color trendscasters.

### 15 Backsplashes

Glass is being used more here due to its crisp, clean, minimalistic look, and the fact that it can be made from recycled materials. Glass panels may be lit for additional back lighting and favorite scenes from vacations or almost anything can be projected on the panel. But metal is also slowly gaining ground. Kitchen designer Doug Durbin, owner of nuHaus, likes metal finishes such as mirror-polished stainless steel as a choice that introduces sheen and sparkle.

### 16 Saving Money

The use of the Internet connecting with your appliances will expand, including features such as tracking when a product is faulty or due for repair. This will provide instant cost control for homeowners. When service technicians arrive for their initial visits, they will know what's wrong and have the correct parts to fix your equipment quickly and efficiently.

New high-tech kitchen items are evolving regularly, and designers are constantly on the look-out for ways to integrate them. Whether these options are incorporated into a kitchen sometimes depends on the clients' age group or tech savviness. Some homeowners are fine with a dial and others want touch screens. Designers can find a happy medium as manufacturers continue to produce items that are adaptable to customers' needs, and can use their creativity to take what's on the market and come up with cutting-edge uses.

*Selected as one of the industry's Top Leaders by* Interior Design *magazine, Alan W. Zielinski, CKD, is active within the National Kitchen and Bath Association (NKBA), having served as their 2012 National President and as a current Board member. Zielinski has been a judge for both the NARI Contractor of the Year Award and the NKBA Design Visions Award.*

**Opposite:** The interior renovation, by Joe Franza of Studio Greener and Joe Human of Designs by Human, was designed to bring the dining and living rooms together and replace a galley kitchen with an open plan. Careful thought was given to improve lighting and maximize storage with built-ins (opposite below).

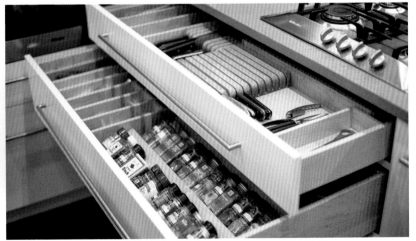

**Warning:**

Avoid making changes once the design is completed and work is in progress unless absolutely critical. "What if" are the two most expensive words in the English language when it comes to remodeling a kitchen. Small tweaks, such as changing hardware or light plates, won't cost much, but adding in a bar sink or more recessed lights, moving a window or increasing its length can make a big difference in the installation schedule and final budget.

**Lesson:**

Unless you're willing to tolerate delays and increased costs, accept the fact that new choices will emerge, but resist them!

**Chapter 7**

# GREAT KITCHENS TO INSPIRE

# SMALL AND BUDGET

**CHALLENGE:** Packing your most wanted features into a small kitchen footprint or one with a tight budget

Good things come in small packages and that applies to kitchens as well. Although it may sound disingenuous, less can be more. Smaller can even offer certain advantages. But in the case of smaller square footage or a smaller budget, you have to prioritize and plan prudently.

This can definitely be a challenge when working within a tighter footprint, but there are clever design ideas that talented kitchen designers and architects use all the time. For example, take advantage of vertical spaces and build cabinets up to the ceiling but have a stepladder handy to reach storage; put movable furniture on casters: tables, butcher blocks, islands, chairs and benches; open up your space with a room that expands into a dining room, family room, even a back porch, or hallway to make a kitchen more functional as a space for large gatherings.

The same holds true for tighter budgets. The smartest professionals know to get you to make choices and go with your biggest wants—a great range, sink, or fabulous backsplash—and then, maybe, scale back on customizing cabinet interiors and exteriors, types of lighting, and flooring.

Bottom line: When thinking smaller, you don't have to skimp on personality and function.

**Previous page:** Lauren Levant Bland of Jennifer Gilmer Kitchen and Bath made separate zones to allow multiple cooks to accomplish tasks. An oversized island houses a drawer microwave and beverage center, and provides prep space. Open shelves float on a paneled wall that is finished with crown molding for a furniture-like feeling. Ceiling beams add warmth. **Top:** "When not in use, make displayed items accessible and create visual layers and pops of color in a small space," says designer Shazalynn Cavin-Winfrey of SCW Interiors. **Opposite:** "Fabric panels—a great alternative to solid cabinetry—provide character and have the added benefit of easily reachable, affordable storage," says designer Cavin-Winfrey. Birch brackets support shelves for open storage carrying through the room's rustic theme.

**Left:** This kitchen, designed by Jennifer Gilmer of Jennifer Gilmer Kitchen and Bath, cleverly utilizes every inch of space. The countertop above the radiator (far right) provides a perch for potted herbs or cookbooks. Holding the wall cabinets a few inches off the ceiling and adding glass inserts on the door panels lightens the cabinets' visual bulk. Removing the soffit extends the cabinetry height and a slim space to the right of the range houses a pull-out spice rack and adds a sliver of counter space for cooking utensils. **Above:** Gilmer extends base cabinetry on the refrigerator wall (far right) to allow room for a second sink and landing space for pans. Deep drawers (to the left of the refrigerator) store dry goods, the cabinet above conceals small appliances and visual continuity is achieved by using the same tile as the sink wall backsplash to wrap the wall above the peninsula.

Multiple use is key. Here are just some ways for each choice to serve multiple needs, an essential ingredient when making selections for a smaller size kitchen or one with a limited budget:

- A dining table can become a writing table or place to put a laptop; a chair or stool may be drafted into service at a bar;

- A counter can become a desk with a stool tucked underneath;

- Appliances can be standard size or even compact so there's more than sufficient room for preparing food and doing other tasks in the same area;

- A peninsula or small island can also house a range, prep sink, or wine cooler to make cooking and entertaining easier and also serve as a place to eat and work. Just be sure that if it's for eating that the counter extends out enough to get stools underneath;

- If there's no room for a traditional island, consider a cart that can serve many of the same functions and top it with butcher block or quartz to serve as an extra prep space.

**Left:** Warm tones of the glass tiles complement the cool tones of the gray cabinets in a kitchen desk area designed by Erica Islas of EMI Interior Design Inc., Los Angeles. **Center:** The U-shaped kitchen, designed by architects Stuart Cohen and Julie Hacker, utilizes the space smartly with an unbroken countertop for food preparation and wall of glass-fronted upper cabinets. The peninsula becomes a casual spot for dining for a family of three. **Right:** After removing the dining room to enlarge a living room, this kitchen, designed by Lisa Wolfe, Lisa Wolfe Design, Ltd, Chicago, had to double as cooking and eating space. The island provides necessary storage and extra counter space, but even better, it has wheels so it's a chopping block near the stove or a dining table pushed against the wall. The large-scale wallpaper pattern helps make the functional space whimsical and gorgeous as well. **Opposite:** Designers Susan Fredman and Aimee Nemeckay of Fredman Design Group in Chicago created a small urban kitchen that delivers all the functionality of a gourmet space, yet intimately, with warm tonality.

**Above:** Sunny yellow sets the tone in this chic ode to kitchens of the past, designed by Jackson Design and Remodeling's Rosella Gonzalez. Retro-inspired buttery yellow appliances also evoke fond memories of Mom or Grandma's kitchen, and yellow on the walls and in various patterns, along with crisp white, make the smallish kitchen appear larger. **Right:** Cheryl Kees Clendenon of In Detail Interiors in Florida used color boldly against a white background to create a lively overall design effect.

Limited size and budget can work together to be the mother of inventiveness. Getting value is the big concern among consumers these days. Here are some ways you can reorganize a tight kitchen footprint and trim your budget.

- Don't feel that the kitchen has to be closed off—people love to know what's going on.

- Use reflective surfaces such as shiny appliances to reflective glass cabinet fronts, mirrored or glass tile backsplashes, plus big windows.

- Whiten, lighten, or bleach all dark wood floors for a fresher look.

- Go in a totally different direction than expected and get bold with color and pattern.

- Use inexpensive but cheerful fabric as cabinet fronts to save money.

- Be a minimalist with collectibles to create a clean, uncluttered vibe.

- Use just one bright color or accessory to spiff up your small kitchen.

- If there's no room for a floating table, tuck a banquette into a corner with a table and chairs or stools that might be able to slide underneath when not in use.

- Use all corners for good storage.

- Replace a traditional door on a pantry or entrance door, which gobbles up space, with sliding, bi-fold, or pocket doors.

- Paint an armoire to match adjacent cabinetry to serve as storage. An open shelf at the top is the perfect perch for cookbooks and collectibles.

- If the kitchen is open to the dining room, use the same flooring to keep the space from feeling boxed-in and tie the two spaces together.

- Have a ledge flip down from an island or peninsula when needed to avoid an expensive separate table purchase.

- Place a sink in a corner of a room to free up more prep space.

- Find a good carpenter or handyman to install shelves to save money or you can choose what you want at a hardware center—cutlery dividers, extended drawers, a trash bin—and that way, you may even be able to install parts yourself.

**Top:** Architect Joe Eisner, AIA, LEED AP, of Eisner Design in New York, wanted a stainless and blackened steel counter to become a serving area for the dining room; it conceals a wine refrigerator behind a blackened steel door. A complementary blackened steel-frame canopy with steel mesh floats above the kitchen and conceals lighting sources. Red lacquer cabinets provide dramatic counterpoint to the dining room artwork. **Opposite:** The small kitchen projects a bold palette of red lacquer cabinets combined with stainless steel appliances. Translucent glass subway tiles separate the stainless steel counter from the upper cabinets.

- Conceal any radiators by building a shelf on top, which can double as a bookshelf or place to grow herbs.

- If your kitchen is also your laundry room, stack your washer and dryer behind bi-fold doors decorated with your kids' artwork or photographs.

- Build in as many appliances as you can to keep them off counters, which may be limited.

"Consider hiring a kitchen designer. An experienced designer can reconfigure any footprint, prioritize needs versus wants, put together the right products without sacrificing style, eliminate mistakes, and save you time and money in the long run," says Gilmer.

**Opposite:** A dark compact island with wood top and distinctive hardware contrasts with the white perimeter cabinets and provides additional storage in this kitchen designed by Jennifer Gilmer of Jennifer Gilmer Kitchen and Bath. **Above:** A built-in dining area makes the most of this space designed by Jennifer Gilmer. The custom upholstered bench offers a comfortable place to gather and complements the custom cabinetry in stained tiger maple with a furniture base and glass doors that provide maximum storage in a shallow pantry.

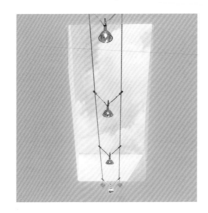

# LONG AND SOMETIMES NARROW

**CHALLENGE:** Designing a long and also sometimes narrow kitchen
to make it functional and look less visually awkward

Long and sometimes narrow is the ideal configuration for a bowling alley and it's also what some small boat owners have to contend with in their kitchens, known as galleys. But on *terra firma*, this is not so perfect. Designing galley kitchens requires extra clever solutions: Locating equipment without walking from one end of the room to the other, having ample counter space and storage, and making sure there's

enough room to pivot about without bumping into someone working on the opposite side can be a real challenge when the available width is small.

The best plans take advantage of length, overcome the narrow width, and disguise its shortcomings with smart choices of materials, colors, patterns, and lighting. Here are more smart tricks to fool the eye:

**Top:** A system of suspension wires solves the problem of getting light to where it's needed most in this Jennifer Gilmer-designed kitchen.
**Opposite:** The island provides multiple functions with another work counter and second sink. It also breaks up the length of the room to make it more inviting.

## Maximize the Positive

A highly functional island can connect two sides of a long kitchen if there's room. Installing an island can utilize space for storage and work surface, include equipment, and use the same cabinetry as the rest of the space for cohesiveness. This is the approach designer Jennifer Gilmer took in a long 19-foot (5.8 meters) kitchen that did not have enough width at 12 feet (3.7 meters). In order to design the island with ample width, she bumped out the front of the house with a box bay window. She placed the main sink on the inside wall, the cooktop in the new box bay facing the front of the house, and on the island included a small wine cooler at one end, a bar sink, and plenty of other storage all around. Because of the room's depth, she had leftover space at a far end to include a small table for four, in what was previously the original kitchen. At 17 feet, or 5 meters at its tallest point, the ceiling was incredibly high and unevenly pitched, making the room feel even narrower and longer. Gilmer lowered the peak to 12 feet (3.7 meters) and rearranged the pitch to ensure the ceiling was better proportioned. On the window side, she also ran cabinetry into the angled ceiling to match the cabinet height on the opposite side. By stringing cable lighting horizontally, the room appears wider and less towering. Other helpful touches include big windows, white walls, and mother-of-pearl, soft green/gray granite countertops.

**Opposite:** To make space for a centered island in a narrow space, the front of the house was bumped out to create a rectangular bay that contains the cooktop. **Top:** Flanking the main sink, tall, deep pantries have bi-fold doors on the center section that help keep the passage unobstructed and an island offers supplemental workspace. **Bottom:** On the opposite wall, the cooktop is nestled in the new bay window and on each side is a stack of drawers with laminated glass-paneled wall cabinets centered above the bay and atop the pantries. Designs: Jennifer Gilmer

**Above:** Orren Pickell broke up a long kitchen with an island in a different material—knotty oak. **Opposite:** Designer Diane Bishop opened up a long plan with a skylight and multiple windows.

Chicago builder Orren Pickell also used a large 10-foot-6-inch-by-3-foot (3.2-by-1-meter) island (opposite) to provide an extra work surface with prep sink as well as a connector between the two sides of a kitchen in a traditional brick and limestone suburban home with French Provincial detailing. To make the island more functional, Pickell, working with Thomas Sarti Girot Interiors, left one end open for cookbooks and surfaced the top in Verde Butterfly natural stone with an eased edge and the base in OP Signature Line cabinetry with beadboard doors in knotty oak with a custom stain.

Though long but hardly narrow at 17 feet (5 meters) wide, this suburban Philadelphia kitchen (above) didn't have enough wall space because of large doors leading to a terrace. Designer Diane Bishop cleverly found more workspace by installing an apron-style sink, dishwasher, microwave, and storage in the island, plus seating on the side facing the cooktop. To open up the room even more, Bishop installed a skylight with clerestory windows right above the island, mimicking its exact shape.

## Play with Color

Color can be used to widen a space, or at least not make it look even narrower when dimensions pose a challenge. It can also be used to divide up a very long expanse as well as separate different functions. Gilmer took this approach in a 22-by-8-foot (6.7-by-2.4-meter) wide kitchen in a high-rise building (above) by using modern, high-gloss white laminated cabinets along one wall and for the base units across from it, but broke up the length with upper cabinets made of engineered rift oak wood cabinetry with grain running horizontally by the cooktop and sink and for a storage hutch at one end. Excessive cabinet details would have cluttered the room visually, so she used slab doors with flush pulls and minimal hardware on the appliance wall.

Designers Terri Crittenden and Aimee Nemeckay of Susan Fredman Design Group Ltd. in Chicago also used color to offset a room's long, narrow shape but in a different way—with black for base and gray for upper cabinets on one side and the exact opposite combination on the other. But on both sides, the countertops are Orion quartzite, the backsplashes are a glass linear mosaic for unity, and the refinished oak floors keep all light and airy beneath. "To offset the length, we separated some of the functional aspects of the kitchen—including the range and refrigerator," says Nemeckay. The kitchen won an award from Thermador for best kitchen.

**Opposite:** White base cabinets contrast with horizontally grained rift oak wall units. Gilmer uses minimal wall cabinetry and floating shelves to add to the spaciousness. **Top left:** High-gloss white base cabinets run the length of the sink wall and seem to float above the dark wood floors thanks to the black toe kick. Gilmer uses the same recessed stainless steel pulls for the base and the wall cabinets to unify the kitchen. **Top right:** Susan Fredman Design Group designers found that different colors can introduce oomph in a long layout.

## Break Up the Space

Sometimes the best way to improve on the challenges of a long and narrow space is to divide it into sections, depending on how long it is. Even a slight increase in counter depth can create the sense of a separate zones within a room while adding valuable counterspace, as Gilmer did in a very long 30-foot (9 meters) kitchen which is only 8 feet 6 inches (2.6 meters) at its widest points. She angled and lowered the desk counter, pulled out countertops by the range and by the breakfast bar to set them apart. At the end of the room, she used dark stained cherry cabinetry to form a tall storage/hutch unit to match the room's base cabinetry that helps move the eye through the entire space. This expansive feeling is enhanced by using a mirrored backsplash between the base and glass-fronted wall unit that comprise the hutch. The other end of the room has glass French doors to a small sunroom with an arched mirrored detail above them to provide reflection and create the illusion of more space.

A still bigger extension can offer even greater flexibility, which is the route the designers of Drury Design took when they used a peninsula to break up the length of a kitchen-cum-dining room perimeter counter (opposite left).

**Above:** To create distinct zones in this narrow space, Gilmer varied the cabinetry color and the depth of the countertops to define the cooking zone, clean-up area, and eat-in bar. **Opposite top left:** A peninsula, even small, can also make space look wider, as seen in this Drury Design kitchen. **Opposite top right:** Designer Sarah Barnard made a traditional galley kitchen seem wider by opening it at one end to views and adding a pass-through.

## Open up Space

In its most traditional format, the long, narrow kitchen can seem hemmed in and offer few options. But by opening it to an adjacent room with a door and pass-through, Los Angeles designer Sarah Barnard avoided making it feel limited or look dark (above right). She used light maple cabinets above and below and faced some in glass, used a polished granite for countertops, and the same pale maple flooring that runs through the rest of the beach-facing apartment.

Recessed lighting and open shelves above the countertops for dishes and collectibles that you want to display will keep a long, narrow kitchen from feeling boxed in and claustrophobic. In many rooms of this configuration, all the cabinets and work areas are placed on one wall and you could choose cabinets that go up to the ceiling and furnish them with pull-out shelves. On the other wall, you have room to set up a banquette, narrow table, or a movable work island.

## Keep It Simple

Avoid large, bold patterns and overly bright colors in a long or narrow kitchen, which will only amplify its challenges. Neutral colors—in this case white cabinets with glass fronts—are smart with some variation for visual interest. "Go simple on the door styles—with fewer lines and here just a slab door, though a Shaker door with simple detail such as a square edge would work and no moldings," says Mariette Barsoum, owner of Divine Kitchens in suburban Boston. Minimize window treatments to let in as much natural light as possible. If you need privacy, consider narrow blinds or translucent shades to let some light in and still maintain privacy.

**Other ideas to keep a kitchen simple:**

**Limit** accessories and small appliances on display;

**Organize** the laundry, pantry, and storage closet into one clean wall of cabinets at one end of the kitchen;

**Eliminate** wall cabinets and in lieu of this, have tall storage at one end of the room;

**Use** the same color cabinets throughout instead of combining colors, though you may want to use a different finish for the island.

**Provide** good lighting through recessed cans and a pendant or two.

## Consider the Function

Built-in wall ovens and microwaves will conserve space in a narrow kitchen, and many appliance manufacturers have also debuted smaller scaled items for smaller homes and apartments for single homeowners or couples downsizing. With counter space also at a premium, you can install a combination sink-cutting board.

Even dining can become more creative. If you don't have room for an island or traditional table, consider using part of one wall as a banquette and adding a tiny 42 inches (1 meter) in diameter table as designer Shirry Dolgin of ASD Interiors did in a Los Angeles kitchen (above). She pushed the table toward the wall as opposed to floating it because of the banquette seat, and then had more open flow for traffic in the rest of the room. She also used an outdoor fabric for upholstery that would hold up well and be stain- and water-resistant.

By carefully placing equipment, cabinets, and countertops, you can have a stunning, functional kitchen with almost everything you want and need.

**Opposite:** A mostly white palette with accents focuses on functionality in a space designed by Mariette Barsoum. Within drawers and cabinets, Barsoum used inserts to organize everything for neatness, stability, and quick access. **Top:** In this Shirry Dolgin-designed kitchen, pattern on the walls is used discreetly, and a tiny table with lively red chairs all prove that narrow doesn't mean boring.

# WORKHORSES

**CHALLENGE:** Getting a kitchen to hum smoothly and work hard

These are our kitchen's workstations that perform dependably under heavy, constant use. Their purpose has been so deeply entrenched that we often take them for granted.

First, consider the work triangle. Conventional wisdom has stressed the importance of placing major equipment at points of a triangle, and no farther apart than 27 feet (8.2 meters) to help cooks work efficiently. However, kitchens have expanded and, since they often contain multiple appliances, the room may demand more than one triangle—or parts of a triangle. And with more space, more cooks work in tandem, necessitating distinct centers to prep, cook, clean up, and sometimes bake, or mix drinks and serve appetizers. A well-designed workspace will provide each zone with sufficient counter space for equipment, cabinetry for storage, outlets to power appliances, and appropriate lighting.

Second, whether there's extra room or a tight footprint, an island or peninsula can make cooking much easier. Both can house equipment, serve as a spot to set out food to cook or serve, eat at, do homework, pay bills, or simply be a place to come together with friends and family.

**Above:** An oversized island has ample counterspace for food preparation and is a perfect place for guests to linger. **Opposite:** When one island is insufficient, particularly when it houses a cooktop and the room isn't large enough for two, consider a work surface on casters that fits under the island. If the table is 31 inches (78 centimeters) high, it can also be used for dining. Designs: Jennifer Gilmer

In this section, we've included a variety of solutions that showcase how space, cooking, serving needs, budget, and design aesthetic all factor into a host of practical, good looking arrangements.

Because of a structural problem with an exterior wall, the owners of a functioning contemporary kitchen had to remodel. This time, they chose to have the new space mirror their home's French Normandy façade. The kitchen's large footprint was made more open by removing a dividing wall to the family room. Designer Jennifer Gilmer decided not to duplicate the room's former angled island or modern style, using French-country influences and including two separate islands (above).

The smaller island is 48 by 74 inches (122 by 188 centimeters) with a marble top, contrasting wood base, and good storage all around since it serves as additional work surface. It's located near the main sink, range, and wall ovens. The second island is much larger at 42 by 120 inches (107 by 305 centimeters) and was set perpendicularly to the smaller island, ensuring good traffic circulation. Positioned near an existing fireplace, it's a more social hub for casual eating and schmoozing, though it also has a second sink. For visual contrast, the soapstone surface around the sink is surrounded by walnut butcher block on white base cabinets.

The room's long 23-foot (7 meters) length and 20-foot (6.1 meters) width meant designer Jennifer Gilmer could create a center island function for multiple uses: casual eating at one end near twin wall ovens and a prep and clean-up center with sink at the other end, close to the range and refrigerator. For a cohesive style, she used the same honed soapstone on countertops, which she darkened with mineral oil, and the same painted gray cabinetry. Soapstone is non-porous, so it doesn't need to be sealed. Barnes Vanze Architects.

Architect partners and husband-and-wife Stuart Cohen and Julie Hacker also like to rely on the island concept (opposite). They find it makes a homeowner's work easier. It can also do more to improve kitchen functionality and looks, such as:

- Provide a work surface for food preparation, accessible from two sides without installing a second work station in the kitchen's primary circulation area;

- Offer seating for informal meals or a place for friends to visit;

- Create a serving counter for food or drinks;

- Offer room for a second prep sink, dishwasher, under-counter beverage refrigerator, or microwave drawer;

- Serve to divide an open kitchen from eating or sitting areas.

With so many choices for island and peninsula tops, choose according to your budget, type of work you most often perform, and how much maintenance you want to expend on cleaning and overall upkeep. Some materials are indestructible; some quite delicate and porous but gorgeous.

In a small traditional kitchen (above), Bernard Kim, designer at Modiani Kitchens in Englewood, New Jersey, used a combination of countertop materials. The Iroko wood top at the peninsula is much denser than typical butcher block, therefore less porous, and the client loves that it is warm and comfortable on their resting arms. The perimeter is Caesarstone, a great quartz selection because of its maintenance-free properties.

**Opposite:** Island-cum-table in a kitchen designed by architects Stuart Cohen and Julie Hacker and designer Stephanie Wohlner gives room to work and eat. **Top:** Bernard Kim of Modiani Kitchens in Englewood, NJ, loves using more than one countertop selection in the rooms he designs, which separates a work area from the more furniture-quality eating and relaxing area.

The island can become much more than a utilitarian workhorse when dressed up with decorative feet, cabinets, or paneled ends, hardware, handsome top surfaces with edge detail and thickness that matches the island's style, and overhead illumination from recessed cans, a chandelier, or the still popular trio of pendants.

Jennifer Gilmer used full-height doors to give a clean look to the base cabinetry and provide easy access to storage. A wine refrigerator is tucked under the counter so guests can help themselves without getting in the way of a cook or cooks. Previous additions gave this kitchen plenty of floor space, but a brick wall obstructed the work triangle. By removing the wall, the spaces could be unified with walnut for the doors on the base units and floating shelves and narrow storage cabinets on the far wall. A large support post was needed but camouflaged with tall, narrow open shelves.

**Top and bottom:** To keep the area feeling light, white upper wall cabinet doors alternate with acid-etched glass tilt-up doors in this Gilmer kitchen.

# Kitchen Islands

Kitchen designer Chris Berry, ASID, of brooksBerry & Associates Ltd., finds that many clients want an island, but there's no single formula that works, as two of her examples show. She also follows these basic mantras:

### Size
Generally your room should be at least 12 feet (3.7 meters) wide and 12 feet (3.7 meters) long. You'll need a minimum clearance of 42 inches (107 centimeters) all around the island—usually 54 inches (137 centimeters) on a side with stools and 48 inches (122 centimeters) between counters, allowing extra for appliances and door clearances. Islands less than 30 inches (76 centimeters) wide don't function well, especially when a sink or cooktop might be included.

### Scale
Small rooms demand small islands and minimal details. Sometimes the best approach is to have a single level, one material, and few extra details.

### Materials
Surface materials look and function better without seams, but rarely are slabs of neutral stone or manmade (quartz) material available wider than 54 inches (137 centimeters) and longer than 126 inches (3.2 meters).

### Seating
Counter-height stools 24 inches (61 centimeters) high at a standard 36-inch (91 centimeters) high counter work best for both young and old. Bar-height stools require children to "climb up" to sit, but once seated they're at an eye-to-eye level with the cook. Table-height chairs—standard at 18 inches (46 centimeters)—are best with bigger islands of two heights.

### Style and Detailing
The island can become a focal point of the room through the choice of color, material, and style. Often, style inspiration can be found in the architectural detailing of the house and can be used to tie the kitchen into the existing spaces well.

# STYLE MAKERS

**CHALLENGE:** Defining your style in a kitchen design that may reflect your home's aesthetic, incorporate some similarities, or be a polar opposite

Like choices of ice cream, kitchens, too, come in wonderfully different flavors—from classic traditional that connotes another era to more unique Biedermeier, Arts and Crafts, rustic, and cutting-edge modern. With so many options, how do you decide about one kitchen style and whether it should borrow inspiration from your home's exterior, resemble other rooms in your house, be a departure that better meets your cooking and entertaining needs, or perhaps fulfills some decorating fantasy?

Here are some of the most common styles to pique your interest, but know that you can create a totally new one by melding different elements.

**Top:** Designer Lauren Levant Bland of Jennifer Gilmer Kitchen and Bath combined hot-rolled steel cabinet panels with quartz countertops, sleek appliances, and a live-edge wood countertop for a perfect composition in a transitional kitchen. **Opposite:** Barnes Vanze Architects used traditional millwork and coffered ceilings blend with contemporary stainless steel appliances and pantry cabinets to create this transitional kitchen designed by Jennifer Gilmer of Jennifer Gilmer Kitchen and Bath. Marble, 2.5 inches (6.4 centimeters) thick, lines the island's counter atop stained wood base cabinets with matching yet thinner marble on the perimeter and backsplash.

## Transitional

This type of kitchen can be tough to describe, walking a fine line between traditional and contemporary. Designing in this mode is a bit like saying, "If I like it, why not?" It requires a bit more creativity and sense of adventure than going with one recipe, but to look right often demands the help of a skilled designer to mix together disparate materials, details, and colors. The big upside is that it can look right in any style home, and rarely goes out of style.

Consider two examples. The first, a complete renovation designed by Barnes Vanze Architects in cooperation with Jennifer Gilmer Kitchen and Bath, marries classic materials such as marble, dark wood, and time-honored architectural elements—ceiling beams, double-hung windows, base and crown molding, and glass-fronted cabinets. Yet, it also incorporates a strong dose of modern touches in its choice of stainless-steel equipment, modern-shaped hood, and cutting-edge pendant lights and hardware. A transitional kitchen can be more modern or more timeless depending on the materials and details. This white kitchen leans toward more traditional, but, has modern twists such as the stainless steel wall of refrigerator/ freezer and pantry, the modern gooseneck style faucets and squared-off cabinet handles.

**Opposite:** Stainless steel ovens are mounted at counter height with glass front shallow wall units above, leaving a shallow counter above in this transitional kitchen. The lantern-style pendant adds a new look to an old style. **Above:** The appliance garage has a bi-fold door that slides out of the way to allow the toaster oven to glide out on a rollout shelf, eliminating countertop clutter in this design by Jennifer Gilmer

This beachfront kitchen also by Gilmer, veers toward a modern vibe with a strong introduction of Far Eastern aesthetic. The Asian touches come from shoji-screen and frosted-glass cabinet fronts, rich walnut wood cabinets, and a 4-inch (10 centimeters) thick by 72-inch (1.83 meters) diameter walnut butcher block dining table top. The modern edginess comes from the display shelves which are open to the dining room, glass mosaic tile backsplash in the current vogue of horizontal tiles laid in a brick (subway) pattern, and wide open vistas into the open-style family room and beyond to the outdoors. The cloth covered traditional chairs and pendant lights are more traditional, which softens the contemporary styling.

**Top:** Frosted glass on some of the uppermost doors lightens the dark walnut cabinetry. Thin mullions evoke shoji-screens and hide what's inside. **Right:** A movable walnut dining table is tucked over the island counter and offers casual seating for two, but it can be rolled into the dining space to seat six when the need arises. Floor-to-ceiling sliding glass doors (on the left) hide an extensive pantry. Designs: Jennifer Gilmer

## Traditional

Traditional kitchens come in countless guises and also have enduring cachet. Most are designed in neutral palettes with long-standing signature materials of wood, marble, and stainless steel; and some detailing at the floor or ceiling with molding, and in cabinet door trim. How much will determine whether it's a classic, purist look with fewer fussy details versus a more defined style such as French or English country, Italianate, or Asian.

Take a kitchen inspired by the Biedermeier style, prevalent in Europe circa 1815 to 1848. It was noted for being a simplified interpretation of the French Empire Napoleonic period, though today it looks anything but simple with fine cabinetry craftsmanship in light native woods with dark accents with minimal ornamentation, and restrained geometric shapes, including curves. Gilmer employed this style incorporating two separate islands for prep (opposite), one doubling as prep and clean-up and the other serving as a breakfast counter. The large size of this kitchen needed better traffic flow from one side to the other, thus the two islands. To achieve the period look, she detailed cabinets in book-matched Sycamore veneer with black painted accents, added some subtle curves to cabinets and countertops, and gave the island base cabinets classic Biedermeier columns.

**Opposite:** Book-matched Sycamore cabinetry trimmed with black accents defines this Biedermeier kitchen. Large enough for two massive islands that markedly improved the traffic flow, curves were added to some base cabinets, the countertops, and trim to soften the look without becoming overly ornamental. **Top left:** A black iron potrack defines the sink island. **Top center:** The breakfast island has a raised platform for comfortable seating while decorative legs and dark bun "feet" add a furniture quality to the ends of the island in this kitchen. **Top right:** Wall cabinets flank a tall window that frames a view of the outdoors. Gilmer added the decorative curve above the wall cabinets to extend visual continuity.

A different but still traditional kitchen was influenced by the Arts and Crafts period, which was spawned in Europe in the late 1800s, originally by artist William Morris. It found its way to America where artists like Gustav Stickley tweaked it into what's known as the Craftsman style, which still resonates with homeowners today because of its prevalence of natural wood materials in soft hues, nature-inspired muted colors, and handcrafted items like wrought-iron handles and ceramic tiles.

In this kitchen, designer Gilmer added a few curves for visual interest, metal accents on the range hood, a dark accent in the granite and walnut countertops, leafy tiles behind the cooktop, and pale green painted walls. When designing a period style kitchen, it's important to keep details in mind so the end result feels authentic and complete. For instance, the hardware is handmade out of genuine hammered copper with a patina for an aged look and the textured glass resembles 1800s glass.

**Top:** Warm wood millwork and cabinetry, open shelving, and beadboard on the back of the peninsula all contribute to the Craftsman look in this kitchen. Framing the arched windows in matching millwork and using aged copper handles and pulls add to the look.
**Opposite:** Here, Gilmer used a stainless steel apron front sink and industrial cooktop to add a contemporary flair that contrasts with the handmade tile mural behind it. Modern slim pullouts above the counter on either side of the cooktop keep spices close at hand.

Traditional can also be interpreted in other ways that lack a definitive peg: a kitchen with a mansard range hood; extra thick doors with a recessed center panel for an old fashioned-style cabinetry feel; oil-rubbed bronze bin pulls, 5-inch (13 centimeters) diameter turned columns, and harlequin-style backsplashes. One kitchen has dark walnut cabinetry with some carved detailing to match the existing dining room armoire and Victorian-style bin pulls and knobs. Another has mostly white with black accents for a French-cum-American twist, which is always a winning combination. Details include a plankboard backsplash, pot rack *à la* Julia Child, oiled soapstone countertops, and French-inspired toile-printed fabric for shades, all of which were selected by the homeowners' interior designer, Helen Sullivan. This circa 1900 house had a large fireplace in the kitchen, most likely for cooking, which set the tone for Gilmer's design direction. She retained the fireplace and used it for the new cooking area and the old chimney now houses the exhaust for the hood. The homeowners found an old fireplace summer cover, original to the house, in their basement. Gilmer decided to use the summer cover as the backsplash behind the range putting it permanently in connection with the fireplace. An existing small window was almost covered up since it looks into the back stairway. Gilmer wanted to keep as much of the original house as possible and designed a pantry with wire inserts to sit beneath it and blend with the age of the house.

**Opposite:** Dark stained wood base cabinets form the island, which has hefty, turned furniture-style legs. To add to the traditional feel, white cabinetry around the perimeter is warmed by faux painted walls continuing onto the modern industrial range hood, which is softened by the crown molding and arched trim. The harlequin pattern backsplash confirms the traditional aesthetic. **Top:** Gilmer eschews wall cabinets to leave the windows as open as possible. Open shelves backed with beadboard and an ultra-wide black iron potrack supply necessary storage. To avoid interference with the original window trim, the soapstone countertops and sink get just a hint of a backsplash.

### Rustic or Country

Some traditional kitchens veer more toward country and even rustic, which visually connotes instant warmth, down-home goodness, and comfort food. They do this by bringing together lots of wood, usually dark stained, in cabinetry, flooring, countertops, and sometimes ceiling beams, plus stonework, and comfortable upholstered seating. To work well, they need good lighting so they're not dark and oppressive, and some colorful touches in decorative details and kitchen accessories.

**Opposite:** To fashion a mountain look in a home in Lake Tahoe, Nevada, designer Linda McCall of Decorating Den Interiors chose quartzite for the floor, native granite for the walls, leathered granite for the island, and polished granite for the perimeter countertops, all offset by warm wood on cabinets and beams. **Left:** Fresh limes, blues, and yellow perk up a casual country-inspired open-plan kitchen and family room—once separate spaces—in this Newport, Rhode Island kitchen, designed by Feinmann Inc.. Whites add updated freshness in the subway tiles, painted cabinetry and ceiling with a pale wood floor. **Above:** Katja van der Loo designed a kitchen in pale gray, the new neutral, to complement a renovated barn's restored beams and walnut cutting board. Small ceramic tiles with a pearly glaze along the backsplash add some glam to the rustic mode.

## Contemporary and Modern

To give your kitchen a lively fresh start, consider modern with its clean spare lines in cabinetry and furnishings, metal and stainless steel finishes, cooler colors or crisp white, and updated appliances and light fixtures.

Gilmer went down this road for her own kitchen with dark cabinets in two different woods—engineered Macassar ebony and painted black refrigerator and accent cabinets—with long sleek stainless steel pulls, honed Absolute black granite countertops, cabinets up to the wood trim around the room, and starkly modern posts and beams, clad in reclaimed oak for some ceiling interest.

**Opposite:** Mixing open shelves, Shaker-style paneling, Iznick tiles, and an abundance of glass and light, this kitchen, designed by Feldman Architecture and Lisa Lougee Interiors, thoughtfully inserts an elegant modern sensibility into an old San Francisco Victorian house. **Above:** In this condo set amid a golf course, designer Judy Underwood of Decorating Den Interiors in Bonita Springs, Florida, used multiple colors of glass tile on backsplashes and in crushed glass set in epoxy for countertops, plus black painted wood cabinets, to fashion a bold contemporary vibe to what had been a kitchen with a Tuscan vibe.

The house was a 1928 traditional Sears & Roebuck bungalow in need of repair. "We thought that we'd need to keep with the traditional bungalow look throughout the house when we decided to renovate it, even though we would rather have had a contemporary house. With the help of Amy Gardner, FAIA, we were able to make the front of the house look like a Japanese tea house, still honoring the bungalow look but then were able to go very modern for the addition at the back of the house," Gilmer says. "This allowed us to design a contemporary kitchen. We decided to keep our wood choices darker because this is in keeping with a traditional bungalow interior. With all the very large glass doors to the outside, light was not a worry. For the evening, we added in a light green back painted glass backsplash, which glows when the hood light is turned on. The old kitchen became the butler's pantry in which we used paneled doors (unlike in the kitchen), which eases the transition from the traditional living/dining areas to the contemporary kitchen/family room area."

Top left: Jennifer Gilmer renovated her own home with the help of architect Amy Gardner, FAIA, and repurposed the original kitchen into a multifunctional butler's pantry with sink, coffeemaker, under-counter icemaker, beverage refrigerator, and dishwasher. Top right: In Gilmer's own home, floor-to-ceiling glass doors allow natural light to flood the Great Room and the kitchen. Opposite: Gilmer designed her own contemporary kitchen with flat, slab doors in wood veneer. Beams overhead repeat the wood's warmth. The oversized range hood makes a bold statement.

# WHITE WINNERS

**CHALLENGE:** Crafting an all-white kitchen for a fresh clean backdrop requires deftness to avoid sterilility

Like the little black dress, a white kitchen can take you anywhere. It's neutral, versatile, and the perfect foil for gleaming appliances. It also gives the illusion of a larger, purer space, especially important for a small kitchen that wants to live large. But too much white can make a kitchen look clinical. While that look was popular in the 1970s when high-tech boldly emerged, it quickly faded in popularity because it connoted coldness and was not as comfortable as a welcoming gathering hub.

The good news is that a white kitchen can be as interesting as any other color setting, but to make it look homey and lived in requires the art of layering different whites to avoid visual monotony.

Paint manufacturers offer a range of shades, such as Simply White, Cloud Cover, Gray Mist, Floral White, White Dove, Ballet White, and Cotton Balls and many cabinet manufacturers now offer to finish cabinetry to match any paint color for a fee. For countertops and backsplashes, consider the array of white marbles that have never gone out of style—Thassos, Calcutta, Glass White, Carrera, and Statuario Venato. And then there are white ceramic and porcelain tiles, white stains for cabinets and wood flooring, glossy white lacquered paint finishes for cabinets, and even bulbs that emit light ranging from warm to cool, and imitate natural white daylight.

**Top:** Sturdy polished nickel pulls blend with the grey veining in the marble countertop and white Shaker inset door cabinetry in this kitchen designed by Jennifer Gilmer of Jennifer Gilmer Kitchen and Bath. **Opposite:** Pulling out the sink base cabinet, inserting a furniture-style one, adding fluted overlays, then topping the marble counter with a classic bridge faucet all work to complete this classic look by Gilmer. Turned legs and beadboard support a butcher-block countertop.

Fortunately, with myriad variations and detailing, there are infinite ways to transform a bland white room into a space that has a unique personality: old-fashioned, traditional, country, transitional, and, of course, contemporary. In one mid-Atlantic kitchen, Jennifer Gilmer painted flat-panel inset Premier Custom Built cabinets Dove White, added furniture-style baseboard, beadboard trim, turned legs, and crown molding, plus Crema Marfil (beige-white marble) for countertops, beveled limestone subway tiles for a backsplash, and old-fashioned stainless steel bin pulls and round knobs, all hallmarks of a classic, timeless white style. Another kitchen Gilmer designed along with Chris Snowber, AIA, has a much more rustic farmhouse charm, despite similar white painted cabinets, because of its beadboard ceiling, peaked ceiling, strong warm

wood accents for the flooring and table, painted light Seattle Mist rafters, Caesarstone Haze counter for the perimeter, and a patinaed stainless steel top for the island. Yet a third kitchen—with a big stainless steel refrigerator and freezer, enormous white hood, and white upholstered chairs around an oversized island—comes across very clean and modern because of its streamlined cabinetry.

To avoid visual boredom, there has to be relief from white, whether in small or large doses. In still another kitchen, Gilmer used Statuary marble with large gray swirls on countertops and the backsplash, painted walls Opal Essence, and laid the floor in gray rectangular slate tiles in an offset pattern, all offering contrast to the clean white painted cabinetry.

**Opposite top left:** Repeating elements used in the desk area unify a multifunctional Great Room designed by Gilmer. The crown molding, fluted overlay on the leg supports, beadboard backsplash, and cabinetry style are the same used in the kitchen work area (above right and opposite). **Opposite top right:** Deep cabinets above the built-in refrigerator and stacked wall ovens add symmetry to a main work area. **Above:** A custom-built hood surround adds visual interest in the same kitchen. Stacked glass-fronted cabinets at the ceiling draw the eye up while adding decorative storage.

There are so many other ways to punch up white with colorful accessories—a red or black coffee maker, an orange or green standing mixer, upholstery, shades, lighting, knobs, glass cabinet fronts that reveal colorful contents behind, and big windows that let in the outdoors. Mother Nature is a pro at introducing a rainbow of hues as does food, candles, and fresh flowers.

White offers you a blank canvas so your kitchen persona can become as creative as you want. The many benefits of a white kitchen explain its everlasting popularity.

**Opposite:** The family room/dining area's cathedral ceiling with painted beadboard and rafters are balanced by the very clean-lined cabinetry, open shelves with minimal crown detail. Gilmer used a plain stainless steel range hood and patinaed steel island countertop to allow the room's architecture to set the stage. Extending cabinetry along the dining area wall yields plenty of storage with pantry pull-outs flanking the large window. **Top:** The fully integrated refrigerator is tucked in the left corner, convenient to the sink. Two freezer drawers can be found directly opposite in the island. Hamilton Snowber Architects and Jennifer Gilmer, Jennifer Gilmer Kitchen and Bath Ltd.

**Opposite:** Sconces with fabric shades provide a soft element above the sink to offset the cold marble countertops and backsplash in this kitchen. At far right, the refrigerator hides behind a mullioned mirrored door. An open shelf above lightens its visual bulk. **Top:** Interior design by Vivian Braunohler, ASID, Braunohler Design Associates LLC. An island trough sink serves double duty as a prep sink and holds ice and drinks when entertaining. Oil-rubbed bronze pulls and details on the light fixtures add timeless appeal. **Bottom left:** White oak doors, stained to match the floors, conceal clutter and break up the tall white wall in the dining area. **Bottom center:** A pass-through allows guests to be part of the party while staying out from underfoot. **Bottom right:** Open space above the oven cabinets is the perfect spot for displaying rustic pots. Raising the island cabinets on legs makes it look like furniture. Designs: Jennifer Gilmer

**Above:** This traditional kitchen features both English and American designs. The Miele refrigerator and freezer are integrated into a custom armoire with arched door panels in a stained and glazed alderwood. The finish is also used on the raised baking center with side-by-side ovens, designed by Gene Abel, senior designer at Kitchens by Design in Indianapolis. **Opposite:** Designed by Gene Abel, senior designer at Kitchens by Design in Indianapolis, the focal point of the cooking niche in this kitchen is the classical style paneled surround with mantel shelf and pullout spice towers. Countertop materials include the work island's sunflower-yellow glazed tile, walnut butcher block, and perimeter's brushed Costa Esmeralda granite.

# COLORFUL CREATIONS

**CHALLENGE:** Discovering ways to spice up your kitchen with subtle or bold splashes of color

Adding too much color in a kitchen may be daring and risky, according to many real-estate pros. "Go white, go beige; make it appeal to the next buyer," they caution. But color can breathe life and vibrancy into a room, especially a kitchen, which has become a home's liveliest hub. It may well be worth the risk to have green, yellow, or even red cabinets, and who knows—the next buyer may love them.

Here are some ways to help decide how far and how bold to go:

• Take a look at your current surroundings; which colors do you keep repeating? Which do you love? Eye-popping reds, nature's inspiration of cool blues and grays, or very, very soothing sun-softened yellows? Any you seriously dislike?

• Study your wardrobe; that will give you big clues about what you like to wear, daily, more infrequently, or not at all. What colors inspire you?

• Which rooms in a magazine, on TV, and in restaurants make you mentally jot down the hue?

• Do you tend to favor more neutrals, and then like to add a pop of color in the same way you top off a neutral outfit with colorful jewelry, a scarf, a tie or a belt?

Now study the colorful examples on the following pages, and see which continue to grab you, after the second, fifth, or even tenth glance.

**Above:** The pale yellow cabinetry was inspired by colors in antique floor tiles that the homeowner purchased in Rome years ago.
**Opposite:** Sinuous curves are used throughout a kitchen designed by Jennifer Gilmer in addition to recessed panel custom cabinets, which were finished in a taupe-gray and lime-green stain that's repeated in the granite. Compatible green glass tiles clad the backsplash in a running bond pattern.

There are many tasteful ways to bring color into your kitchen and have fun with it, whether it's an outrageous all-out feast, or simple peek. Some prefer a dark or a more neutral color scheme. However, some feel that neutral colors give the message of too safe, sterile, and unfriendly. *Au contraire*. Natural wood and wood stains offer color variations that tend to be timeless. These include wood flooring, butcher-block countertops, or perhaps a wooden desktop or chairs. Neutral colors may also be paired with rich woods on countertops, floors and furniture, metallic backsplashes, a patterned fabric on a window shade over a sink and interesting light fixtures, or a bold splash of color on the walls. Subtle and muted accent colors on tile surrounds, wall ovens, or even flooring can also bring in just enough color to make a statement.

**Opposite:** In an historic preservation with beautiful windows that bring in a strong outdoor presence, designer Kristin Okeley, ASID, CKD, wanted the room to reflect a sky-blue freshness through paint. The accent color can easily be changed to perk up the room's timeless palette of white, black, and wood. **Top:** For a vacation home on the Washington coast, designer Garrison Hullinger added vibrancy and light by painting the room a lively green with a pearl finish for sheen. The color also pops against the sanded and painted 1980s oak cabinets, and porcelain-tile paved floor.

For those willing to take a more colorful risk, use a bold color in the cabinetry, but balance it with different colors on the island, floor and backsplash as designer Jennifer Gilmer and architect Jerry Harpole did in a kitchen that's part of a federal-style home. Gilmer selected an apple-green paint shade to accent the island base because the client had her heart set on a green and taupe gray kitchen, installed similarly colored tiles for the backsplash, and painted the walls in their grill room the same hue. So the green wouldn't overwhelm the space, she used gray/green granite for the island countertop; painted perimeter cabinets in a light taupe gray; installed big skylights overhead and large windows, and plenty of various light fixtures; and laid an oak floor to match the existing floors in the home.

Gilmer used a more subtle, yet still colorful, approach in a small kitchen that is open to the breakfast and bar area. The yellow cabinetry immediately perks up the traditional space with its bold green range. Walls clad in slate are contrasted with more formal walls that are faux painted off white and silver vines. Using the client's 18th-century Italian tiles as a runner bordered with a light terra cotta floor, she fashioned a warm, European-inspired kitchen, adding turned posts above the refrigerator and as supports below the counter for a handcrafted feel. Gilmer used polished granite for the countertops, left many wall cabinets open to mimic furniture and to display colorful dishes and serving pieces.

**Right:** Curved front cabinetry adds an interesting design element and disguises the exhaust system. It also permits display space for crockery. Using one color family—green in this case—requires a deft balancing act to avoid monotony. Gilmer used the darkest, richest green on cabinets, lightened it up for glass backsplash tiles, and chose a speckled granite for countertops. **Opposite:** Sunshine yellow warms up a small but very welcoming kitchen. The peninsula has been finished with a soft curve to offer enough space for a breakfast bar, which Gilmer topped with polished granite to add a modern contrasting element.

## Do's and Don'ts of Mixing Colors

**Try** to find one item you'd like to incorporate in your kitchen that has colors you can pull from. In the case of a yellow Gilmer-designed kitchen, the client brought in tiles that she imported from Italy, which gave the designers a great palette as a starting point.

**Use** your favorite color as the accent color, or use one that already exists in your home. You can use this for the backsplash, wall paint color, or interior cabinet paint color. It's always a bonus to find plates or art work with the same or a complementary color that you can display to create a cohesive look.

**Find** a painted piece of furniture to incorporate into your kitchen, whether one you have or one you discover at a furniture store or antique market. This can be the starting off point to create your color palette and you can get samples of cabinets, counters, tiles, and flooring materials that complement it.

**Make** sure to create a balance with the different colors. Try to incorporate the prominent accent color in three places, fairly evenly spaced apart from one another. Three places are always a good balanced number and will keep you from overdoing the color. Don't be afraid to use a different color for one centerpiece, like the range or the hood or even the counter stools.

**Opposite:** CG&S Design Build in Austin designed and built a kitchen for a homeowner who was closely involved in remodeling her entire house. For the kitchen, color expert Louise McMahon of Perfect Palette selected an apple-lime green for the cabinets and vivid red for the backsplash. **Above:** To have a butler's pantry that would become a connecting link to the kitchen, dining room, and guest bathroom, architect Sheri Newbold, owner of Live-Work-Play in Seattle, designed it as a wide space to walk through but also serve as an attractive area to hang out for drinks. The blue-green painted cabinets repeat a kitchen color; storage was custom designed to be functional and attractive; and good lighting in cabinets and overhead make it cheerful.

**Top:** Sol Quintana Wagoner, a designer at Jackson Design and Remodeling in San Diego, made a new kitchen full of vibrant color, engaging textures, and an appealing blend of cultural influences. The orange paint color complements the peninsula, fashioned from apple-green Caesarstone and rustic wood with a natural edge. **Above:** In the same kitchen, a custom backsplash shimmers with shades of violet, orange, and copper mirror and apple green and became a defining inspiration for all the kitchen's colors, which evokes the home's Spanish roots. **Opposite:** The clients wanted to use a fire-engine paint chip but designer Jason Landau, owner of Amazing Spaces LLC, steered them to a softer timeless red, "as timeless as red can be," he says. He used a stain that allowed wood grain to show through, and to tone it down paired it with white Carrera marble countertops, a black painted island, and porcelain tile flooring.

WOLF
Dinner
@
7pm
Grocery store:
milk
bread
ice cream
olive oil

**Opposite:** Senior designer Nancy Stanley of Kitchens by Design in Indianapolis and her clients fell in love with slate tiles in a range of natural colors for the backsplash, then pulled one of the greens to match for the cabinets. She added a dark green contrast in the Soapstone countertop. **Above left:** To ease the transition between the old and new parts of a kitchen, Gilmer used a curved cabinet to conceal the slight misalignment in the wall. **Above right:** When designer Claudia Juestel of Adeeni Design Group was asked to brighten a white and beige kitchen so it would be a "happier" space, she worked up four custom yellow shades with a brown glaze that would appear a bit muted and aged. The result: the right level of brightness and cheerfulness without being garish.

Want your kitchen to introduce color more delicately? Try putting color into the parts of the room and accessories that are easier to switch out if you get bored.

- Add color with glass or metallic tiles, on backsplashes, or countertops or get creative with colorful knobs or pulls.

- Put color into your choice of stools, fabrics, small appliances, dish towels, utensils, a clock, a blackboard used with colorful chalk, kids' artwork in colorful frames, or a pantry door painted in a contrasting hue.

- Paint walls, or try paint or wallpaper on the ceiling.

- Add color through your choice of lamps, switch plate covers, shades, and even bulbs; enhance these by putting them on dimmers so the color varies even more.

Go ahead and have fun with color to create a unique space that makes a statement about who you are.

**Right:** With interior design help from Mitchell Manning Associates, designer Julia Kleyman of Ulrich Inc. personalized a classic white kitchen by introducing blue upholstery, patterns, and a painted ceiling. **Opposite top:** In a kitchen designed by Katie and Ruben Gutierrez of Errez Design, a yellow wallpapered ceiling adds oomph where least expected. One plus of this strategy is that the paper stays fresh and clean since it won't be affected by wet, dirty, or greasy fingerprints or cooking oils. **Opposite bottom:** In a modestly scaled kitchen, certified master kitchen and bath designer Wendy Johnson of Designs for Living Inc. added some square footage and a family room. Johnson picked a soft fresh green and contrasted it with purple stools for punch. The countertops are classic for the home's Connecticut locale—white marble and white subway-tiled backsplash.

# Picking Kitchen Colors

There are so many important decisions to make when you design your kitchen—deciding on appliances, task areas, and cabinetry for storage. Often your last decision is ironically what you see first when you walk into the room—the color scheme.

Color selections apply to many areas of the kitchen, including paint and stain choices. Cabinets, countertops, backsplashes, hardware, flooring, and appliances require choosing one color or an array of hues. No choice should be made without considering others, ensuring all the colors are in harmony when the room is complete. Look at the color wheel and pick what makes you happiest. Finding cabinet, hardware, and countertop colors comes more easily once you have a palette in mind.

Choosing the right colors also means creating a sense of balance. One color might define the room, a soft blue, for example, and then all the other colors should complement it. For example, if you are going with a softer blue, you might choose nickel hardware and charcoal gray granite. Clearly, the blue might be used for the wall color, which helps create the room's identity; all other color selections should complement the blue.

Start by setting the stage and decide on the room's identity and mood, which can be expressed not just through colors but also textures and patterns. Is it a room that you want bright and colorful or subdued and understated? Do you want it playful to appeal to children and whimsical adults, or a quiet place to enjoy a glass of wine and read quietly at the end of the day?

## Cabinets

Cabinets make the biggest statement. Since there are often no large comfy couches or brightly colored rugs in a kitchen—though nowadays there can be—the colors of your cabinets should be the first thing you consider. A stained cabinet finish has always been a classic, looking polished and elegant. It's the "furniture" in the room. Painted cabinets have become more popular recently and provide many options—bright white for a more contemporary look or creamy beige for a more timeless or vintage appearance are safe, universally appealing options. Lacquered cabinets in either selection create a more contemporary look and are appealing in many high-end environments. Even a dramatic red or apple green may appeal to some who like a more energetic approach. Whatever color you choose, the mood should also convey crisp cleanliness and efficiency since a kitchen is a place where you work.

## Flooring

A brighter floor will jump out at you, whereas a more subdued color will be more background filler. I like colors that grab your attention to be higher in the room rather than drawing your eyes downward. If you choose wood flooring, it should either contrast with cabinets or match—avoid a color that is close but does not match exactly, since it will end up looking like you tried to match but missed.

## Countertop

The counter color serves several purposes. Firstly, it is where you look when you are working so it needs to be easy on your eyes. Some people find the blackest granite, soapstone, or quartz counter tiring but enjoy a bold contrast with a lighter cabinet choice. There are some velvety grays available that can make a strong statement without harsh visual contrast.

Secondly, the countertop gives you the opportunity to add a wonderful accent color to your room, often at its center. For example, if you use stained cabinets, adding beautiful wood tones to the room, or brighter white or off-white cabinets against a quieter floor color, the countertop can be where you add a wonderful, zesty pop of color.

## Walls

In most kitchens, there is usually only minimal wall space for color because of appliances, backsplashes, windows, and doors. Here are some rules of thumb: With cabinets that are close to, if not touching the ceiling, add saturated wall color in the blank areas, if you have a brighter color cabinet a softer wall color would be better as it would not compete with the cabinet color. Use a lighter wall color for a wood stained cabinet since the wood can stand out nicely against the rich wood tones. If you would normally choose beige, move it up one notch to a warmer caramel. If you love a fresh spring-like green, make sure it is bright enough to create the mood you want rather than washed out. You can use colors inspired by your small appliances, too—a yellow or pink standing mixer—or from your dishes or favorite placemats and napkins. Or, merely select a color that makes you feel cheerful. When it comes to picking the finish—matte, semi-gloss, gloss, high-gloss, or lacquer, think about upkeep since some are easy to wipe clean or reflect more light and dirt than others.

## Ceiling

Frequently called the fifth wall in the room, the ceiling can blend in with the trim color in the room or be an accent color. Think about matching your cabinets if they are a painted white or off-white. If your cabinets are wood, the ceiling should match the room's painted trim color. If you want an accent color, then a creamy beige or soft blue or gray—a popular hue—creates a pleasing mood for the room. Most important is that the ceiling should not be a bold color that stands out; instead, it should complement the cabinets and wall color. Matching trim or going with a subtle accent color are the best choices.

## Finishes

When choosing finishes for your kitchen, remember this is a room where the walls will be exposed to moisture, heat, smoke, and a range of temperatures. You want whatever you bring into the room to remain durable for as long as possible. When you choose your paint selection, be specific about ordering the right quantity. Talk to a paint expert and explain you're buying for a kitchen. Describe equipment choices and how the room will be used. Different companies also have their own finishes, so share as much information as you can and get quotes on different manufacturers' lines, since prices also vary.

## Sense of balance

Before you are completely finished, know that all the colors mixed together should reflect a sense of balance for the right ambience. If you're seeking a friendly, inviting space, all the colors and combinations should be upbeat—perhaps warm yellow or fresh green. If you want it a bit romantic at night with lights dimmed low, think about incorporating richer creams, warmer golds, or earthy terracottas. Dark heavy colors— particularly if you're thinking of having dark cabinets, walls, cabinetry, and floors—can be oppressive and unwelcoming. Also, keep in mind that lighting will enhance colors, much like frosting on a cake. With a luster to the cabinets and a shine to your appliances and possibly your countertop, the kitchen is more reflective than any other room in your home. A well-chosen combination of textures and colors enhances the feeling of a clean overall shine.

Choosing your colors wisely reflects your heart and soul. Make this choice as carefully as everything else that goes into your kitchen design repertoire.

*Amy Wax, author of* Can't Fail Color Schemes Kitchens & Baths (Creative Homeowner)*, has more than 25 years of experience selecting colors for home interiors and exteriors, including kitchens.*

# OPEN-STYLE KITCHENS

**CHALLENGE:** Opening up a kitchen to other rooms in a house means blending its style and function with adjoining living spaces

As traditional colonials and ramblers are remodeled and renovated to suit today's active lifestyles, kitchens are being recognized as the nucleus of the home. Originally, the kitchen was completely separate from the living room, dining room, library, family room, outdoors, and other spaces. In the 1950s, some progressive architects began designing so-called "modern" houses with open floor plans, combining the living and dining rooms and opening the kitchen to the rest of the house for efficient family living. In the 1970s, urban centers gentrified former industrial areas to create open lofts for artists and musicians where everything, living and working, took place in virtually the same room. Today, the open plan suits varied tastes and lifestyles, with the kitchen as the hub, and adjacent areas where you can sit, eat, work, or play.

Open floor plans come in many configurations, so choose what works best for you if this style appeals:

- A work area, along with a casual eating space (often at a bar, island, or peninsula) that also serves other functions (additional meal preparation space, study space, or workspace) that is totally open, as it is in a loft, with the kitchen's finishes reflecting other rooms' furnishings, colors, and materials;

- A work area merged with another space for eating or socializing, such as a family room;

- A space delineated from other areas by architectural elements such as beams, vertical columns, built-in furniture, or furniture groupings, and rugs.

**Above:** An oversized island with an integral sink doubles as prep space and a table thanks to generous overhangs on the sides and back. Open to the family room, an unobstructed view of the fireplace and kitchen makes clean-up less onerous. Using countertops and tile in a similar hue makes the space cohesive. **Right:** Removing a wall between the kitchen and family room reduced the number of wall cabinets in this Gilmer project. Storage was gained by installing floor-to-ceiling cabinets that face into the family room and match kitchen cabinetry. A floating shelf in the same wood finish further ties rooms together.

## Go Wide Open

Designer Joe Human of Designs by Human took rooms that once were closed off and crowded with furniture—a small kitchen, dining, and living rooms—and transformed them into one open and modern yet comfortable living area. Within the whole, there are zones for guests and kids while owners entertain or relax (left). Because the ceilings in the existing space also were choppy and created unattractive shadows, Human lowered the heights to a consistent 10-foot (3 meters) level, which made the space look larger. Now, he says, all members of the family can be in separate areas, yet also be together.

Architect Amy A. Alper also knew that a long room configured as separate areas could work better with all the walls down. The modern aesthetic the owners wanted also correlated well with one end for working, a middle section for living, and the other end for eating.

**Left:** Designer Joe Human combined rooms once closed off, yet kept distinct areas for cooking, sitting, and eating. **Above:** In a more modern approach, architects Amy A. Alper and Mark Hummel took down walls in their house, and set aside areas to work, live, and eat.

**Top:** Using similar materials—in this case, Douglas fir wood—unifies the different functions of one big open room, designed by architect Phil Rossington. **Above left:** An open-style kitchen may involve different functions, depending on how a family lives. Here, designer Susan Dowling nestled a sitting area by a window. **Above right:** In another Dowling design, an island separates work and sitting areas.

A kitchen designed by architect Phil Rossington of Rossington Architecture uses the same vertical grain Douglas fir wood throughout (opposite top) to unify its different functions, and only forms minimal separations—a counter to hide working clutter of the kitchen, and a wood screen to define the entry and obscure views from the front door. The cabinetry continues into the dining and living areas, ties them together, and adds tranquility to the large open space. Because good lighting is critical in a larger area, Rossington used a skylight to wash the kitchen with natural illumination which also has the effect of adding vertical height.

## Merge a kitchen with one area for socializing or eating

Sometimes, just one additional function makes sense, as designer Susan Dowling of Susan Dowling Interior Design found for two different families, each of whom wanted to be able to socialize and have the kitchen totally within view. With one in Amelia Island, Florida, just north of Jacksonville, the sitting area is small, nestled in front of windows in a bay. The homeowner wanted to have family near while she prepares meals, so she opted for casual dining at the island and comfortable upholstered seating in the bay with a wall-mounted TV. In the second kitchen in Atlanta, Georgia, Dowling increased the

sitting area, anchoring it by a stone fireplace, and creating a division between rooms with a change in ceiling height and by separate Oriental rugs (opposite bottom right). The homeowners are both tall, so they raised the island height, which allows the dishwasher to be up higher for easier use.

Interior designer William Caligari of William Caligari Interiors combined his working and eating functions in his own kitchen (above left). Because formal dining rooms are rarely used as they were in the past, he transformed his into a library off the kitchen. The kitchen now combines cooking and eating spaces, which works when he and wife, Pascale, cook and eat with family. If they have guests and are busy preparing and serving food, they can now interact with them. Because Caligari wanted the kitchen to be light and bright, most of the cabinets, counters, walls and light fixtures are chalk white, a counterpart to two walnut cabinet pieces he designed for the cooking wall and interior of the upper cabinets that is slate blue. The pantry armoire and upper cabinets all have glass doors for visibility. "People think china, glassware, and food supplies need to be hidden, but it depends on what you own," he says. "What we have in our cabinets for dry goods looks great, along with our china, glassware, and kitchenware, so why not see everything!"

**Top left:** In designer William Caligari's home, he melds cooking and eating functions. **Top right:** Designer Elizabeth Tranberg left room in a big open kitchen for a choice of dining spots.

Space for a large eating area in the kitchen promotes conversation and coming together without affecting the flow of the work space, the approach Elizabeth Tranberg of The Kitchen Source, took in a kitchen (p.167). The delineation created by the architecture of the home into the living room instills a sense of separation and creates visual interest. At the same time, it allows for cohesiveness between the two spaces and an open feel when it is a casual setting while, at the same time, creates formality when a more structured gathering occurs.

Shazalynn Cavin-Winfrey of SCW Interiors used a large island to create a boundary for the open-style kitchen and family room (right). The same pattern on the walls is used throughout the space, creating a sense of continuity, which is also important. The large pendant over the island elongates the space.

### Connect the kitchen to another room with a large opening between, but leave some sense of separation

Without walls to separate the spaces, natural light from other rooms spills into the kitchen. Designer Jennifer Gilmer took this approach with two new kitchens. The first, behind a traditional brick façade, features a working space open both to a casual eating room and a large family room. A wall was removed between the kitchen and family room, replaced with floor-to-ceiling cabinetry that creates a clear separation of the two rooms and allows plentiful storage. Gilmer designed a peninsula counter fabricated from 2-inch (5 centimeters) thick Valley Gold marble, which serves as a bar area when entertaining and conveniently houses a beverage center and wine cooler on the kitchen side. A floating shelf and soffit trim were added to make the spaces feel more cohesive. The two rooms share important commonality with walnut wood cabinetry, a dark palette, and contemporary style.

**Above:** White cabinetry pops against a vibrant green backdrop and a cabinet crafted with wood from Indonesian boats adds intrigue and character. A staggered medley of tangerine pendant lights delineates the dining table and distinguishes its space in the open area, designed by Sol Quintana Wagoner of Jackson Design & Remodeling. **Opposite top:** An island can work as a dividing feature, as in a kitchen designed by Shazalynn Cavin-Winfrey of SCW Interiors. **Opposite below:** In a kitchen designed by Jennifer Gilmer, the island becomes an important secondary work surface, close to the sink or any other piece of equipment.

The second was inspired by loft-style living with a nice sized kitchen and oversized island (left). With its overhang on the back and two sides, the island does double duty as the family's kitchen table. The refrigerator was placed next to the main kitchen, in what was the old butler's pantry, to keep the space feeling large and open. Clad in the same tile as the fireplace wall opposite them, the floating shelves flanking the hood offer open storage space. The fireplace wall also has a niche for the TV, that's totally in view from the kitchen, without obstruction.

A third variation on this theme presented a natural demarcation because of a change in grade between the kitchen and adjacent family room. Designer Kristin Okeley of Kitchens by Design (above) played up the rooms' separation by building in a long storage unit between them as a divider and exposing the vertical support ceiling beams overhead.

By following any of these designs, you are likely to make your kitchen and its adjoining areas the most interesting and busiest room in your home.

**Left:** Rustic gray blacksplash tile contrasts smartly with the stainless steel squares above the burners. Open shelves substitute for wall cabinets in this casual Gilmer kitchen that invites diners to pull up a seat at the generous island. **Above:** In an open kitchen designed by Kristin Okeley, stools at the counter inject fun and the feeling of a retro 1950s diner.

# FAMILY-FRIENDLY HUBS

**CHALLENGE:** Making your kitchen a striking but practical hub for all family members

If your kitchen is the hub of your home where everyone hangs out, shouldn't it be designed to accommodate everyone's wishes, including four-legged members? With extra planning for function and good design, your kitchen can be as good as it gets for all.

Before you design a family kitchen, analyze how each member—and their friends—may use the space, and how a multitude of functions can be combined in one footprint without the room or people feeling crowded.

The dream might be a cook's haven to prepare family and company meals, sit and sip a cup of coffee and read the newspaper, or catch up on phone calls from a comfortable perch with outdoor views. It might be a place to unwind at the end of day with a glass of wine, and, on weekends, become a stage for making family breakfasts.

For young children, it could be the spot where they play, do crafts or homework close to a parent; for visiting grown kids, a place to get them to open up about their lives, or simply connect with friends.

**Top:** An oversized island in a Jennifer Gilmer-designed kitchen creates plenty of space for kids to stay outside the work triangle while helping themselves to snacks. **Opposite:** A custom-built hood is suspended over a gas cooktop and leaves the exterior wall of windows unobstructed for the family to enjoy the water view in a kitchen designed by Jennifer Gilmer in collaboration with Wiedermann Architects. The walnut butcher block island top extends down the side of the granite countertop to accommodate seating for seven.

In a kitchen designed by Jennifer Gilmer, the emphasis was on versatility, with an island with stools a few inches higher than the prep area, a separate table, and a pass-through to the family room addition (above). The wall between the dining room and the kitchen was removed to allow space for this island and to give the family a large room to entertain in or to just hang out. The back wall of the dining area is a continuation of the kitchen, with matching cabinetry providing additional storage and a hidden desk behind the unit's center doors. Cork on the back of the desk's doors allows the family to pin up sports schedules, pictures, and anything else that is necessary to have handy.

**Left:** With so many doorways and windows, finding a spot for the refrigerator was a challenge for Gilmer. The solution: hide the 27-inch (68.5 centimeters) wide Sub-Zero refrigerator behind panels (on the left of the main doorway), which allows space for a two-tiered soft-curved bar of beech butcher block in the eating area. Adding a nearby prep sink under the pass-through and an under-counter freezer next to the refrigerator gives homeowners another functional and separate work zone.
**Top:** Using the same rich, dark cherry wood as the cabinetry to frame the pass-through unifies the kitchen and family room. Gilmer continues the cabinetry to the right of the window to provide ample storage and hide a desk area in the center.

Gilmer made this island extra large—6 feet 9 inches by 4 feet (2.1 by 1.22 meters)—for everyone to gather around, topped it with 3-inch (7.6 centimeters) thick Caesarstone, designed open shelves for the family's colorful dishes so everyone can grab what they need, and applied back-painted glass panels in a soft sage color for a cheerful backdrop. The client requested two sinks with only 24 inches (61 centimeters) in between, almost side by side, because she loves to bake, sometimes with the help of her children. This wide-open kitchen has a dining table beyond the island , and, to the left, an area that was furnished for kids and guests to hang out while Mom cooks and bakes.

**Right:** Breaking up a wall of cabinetry with an open shelf and stainless steel appliances keeps this kitchen from being too overpowering, yet allows ample hidden storage.
**Opposite:** In the same kitchen, Gilmer uses back painted glass to create a seamless backsplash to reflect light from the windows that top the countertop beneath the open shelves. The oversized island is a multi-functional space with a tall black toe kick that makes it appear less bulky and more like a piece of furniture. Randall Mars Architects.

So how do all the different family needs get incorporated into the best design?

- Good equipment—and enough of it—because there are often multiple cooks who need to prep, cook, serve, clean-up, but with some separation among different tasks.

- Comfortable and ample seating since enjoying coffee or reading the paper is high on many wish lists. Have a couch or chairs by a fireplace with TV, perhaps, or at least a wide opening to an adjacent family room.

- A counter for kids to work or color on and open floor space for them to play, with a beverage center and microwave drawer close by and shelves or toy bins to hold their books and games.

- Additional counters—maybe one lower if an older family member has mobility issues—and movable seating for when the family expands exponentially.

- A blackboard or corkboard to list activities, a counter with plugs to charge smartphones and tablets; and if there's extra room add a mud room as the place to leave backpacks, coats, and boots, and keep all that out of the kitchen.

- Areas open to the outdoors to bring in views and light, as well as allow for family members to oversee activities.

**Opposite:** To find room for a large family to eat or do homework, designer Christopher Grubb of Arch-Interiors Design Group Inc. creates a big island as the command center, with sink and range nearby. Extending the island top beyond cabinetry creates a place to sit with an overhang at least 16 to 20 inches (40 to 50 centimeters) for knee comfort. Beams on the vaulted ceiling add a warm, intimate cottage feeling. **Top:** For cooking and entertaining, this family wanted an oversized refrigerator, double ovens, a gas range top, and an island, plus a built-in coffee center for the husband and wife. Designer Mariette Barsoum CKD, of Divine Kitchens fits all in, including room for two stools so the children have a place to eat and do homework while their parents prep.

Safety always needs to be factored in, whether a family means one person or many, but it takes on greater importance with children and elderly members. Include good lighting, eliminate sharp corners, cover cords, and perhaps lock drawers and cabinets for medicines or cleaning supplies. A change in color or texture on the floor is wise if there's a step to a different level. Materials should be easy to wipe down and endure wear and tear. You might consider more resilient flooring materials, such as textured cork or rubber. For counters, solid surfaces such as quartz or quartzite are easier to maintain than porous marble. Similarly, semi-gloss

paints and finishes on cabinets and walls hold up better than matte. If you have pets, you might want to install scratch-resistant floors—possibly ceramic or porcelain rather than wood or slate.

And never forget your budget. Not ready to invest in a sofa or upholstered cushy chairs? Add cushions or padded seats to your stools. No room for a table to seat everyone in your existing space? You don't have to move. You may be able to take down a wall that separates the dining room and have one big, combined space.

**Top:** The unusual trapezoid-shaped island in this California coastal kitchen was designed by senior interior designer Tatiana Machado-Rosas of Jackson Design and Remodeling to enhance family togetherness during meals and homework time. **Opposite top left:** Extra square footage allows ample space for a kitchen island that has become the center of activity for this family. Designed by Feinmann, Inc., Designer/Builder, the island has storage, a second prep sink, a Bosch electric cooktop, and a glass hood. **Opposite top right:** In the same kitchen, expanding the space creates a new eating area with a 42-inch (107 centimeters) round table. The sizable gliding and fixed transom windows bring in light and views of the bucolic backyard. **Opposite bottom:** Having as much counter space as possible in an L-shaped work arrangement makes a small kitchen function for a family, even without an island. By relocating laundry equipment, designers Katie and Ruben Gutierrez of Errez Design found a spot for a small breakfast nook. Open shelves are a casual way to display items used daily.

# MULTITASKING MAGICIANS

**CHALLENGE:** Designing a large kitchen to outfit multiple work zones, and a smorgasbord of new kitchen activities

If you are lucky enough to have a large kitchen or are building an addition onto your house, capitalize on its size by making it into a five-star room that carves out distinct work areas for food prep, clean up, and eating—each with vital bells and whistles.

One of the main secrets to a well-orchestrated, busy kitchen is that people don't get in each other's way; someone who wants to pull ingredients from the refrigerator doesn't bump into another who's moving between the prep counter and range to stir dinner ingredients. This doesn't mean ignoring the traditional work triangle, defined by the location of the main sink, range, and refrigerator/freezer. Rather, it arranges equipment, countertop space, and storage in separate work zones. This may mean installing two wall ovens in different places, as opposed to stacking them in a traditional way, for different types of cooking, splitting the refrigerator and freezer into two units to allow for more space in each, or adding an additional sink for specific tasks along with a second dishwasher for party cleanup.

**Top:** Designer Jennifer Gilmer designs a column for wine storage and adjacent open shelves to display collectibles. **Opposite:** In the same kitchen, custom natural cherry millwork unifies a kitchen, family room, and desk area. Wrapping the family room beam and columns and running multi-piece crown molding in both rooms make the space feel cohesive.

## Let's Prepare

Consider a designated prep area where food is washed, cut, measured, and mixed. It should be near a refrigerator, sink, and supplies frequently used, and, if possible, be near a dishwasher or close or adjacent to a cooking center. This is where the cooktop or range is the centerpiece with ample counter space on one or both sides and within reach of storage for pots, pans, utensils, oven mitts, water tap, and safety equipment like a first aid kit and fire extinguisher. If you love to bake from scratch, a baking center might be an additional hub within this zone. Have frequently used ingredients stored near the range along with easy access to utensils, a marble slab for rolling out or kneading dough, and cabinetry with slots for baking trays and cupcake pans. And remember to install a powerful hood, especially if you have a grill.

In some kitchens, there's enough room in square footage and the budget to have multiple ovens, sinks, work counters, beverage centers, and still have room for plenty of storage.

**Opposite top:** Raising the bar counter a few inches helps hide clutter on the sink side from the family room. **Opposite bottom:** Adding cubbies for wine makes use of a space under the countertop. **Left:** Extending the countertop behind the faucet gives generous room for food prep. The cooktop has counter space and shelves on both sides. Separating the oven and cooktop eases traffic jams when multiple cooks get going. Designs: Jennifer Gilmer

## Let's Eat

An eating station, which can be an island or peninsula, a freestanding table and chairs, a wall-mounted table that folds down when not in use, or a built-in banquette, should be close to silverware, glassware, linens, and condiments and, if possible, positioned within view of other work zones.

**Top:** Certified master kitchen and bath designer Wendy Johnson of Designs for Living Inc. gives new meaning to the term multitasking with a serious work space for gourmet cooking and baking and an area to serve drinks complete with a desk, bar with LED lighting that changes color, huge TV, wine storage, and coffee center. **Right:** Designer Lori Carroll of Lori Carroll and Associates makes the view the star in this large kitchen where there's ample counter space for working and setting out food, a rounded built-in table for eating, good equipment, cabinetry, and artificial lights for when the sun goes down.

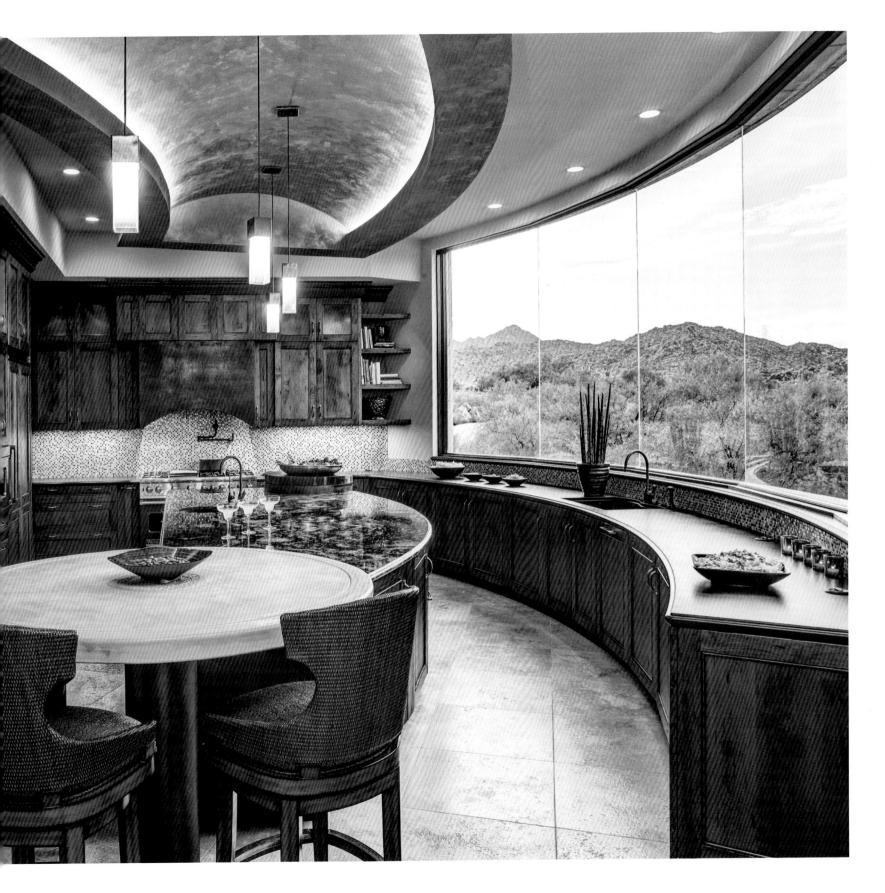

## Let's Clean Up

When planning a clean-up center, consider its proximity to storage for items used in the other work centers with a place for dishwasher soap and towels, with counter space to stack and dry dirty dishes and pans.

**Opposite and top:** Decorating Den Interiors' designer Sandy Kozar's own kitchen opens to a dining room with a big island for entertaining, casual eating, and cleaning up. **Left:** The space includes a coffee center, which designer Kozar built in, along with the adjacent built-in refrigerator/freezer.

## Let's Work and Play

If you have enough space, other work zones might include a bill-paying station with counter space that's rarely used for food preparation, or even a built-in desk, though these are losing popularity as computers get smaller and wireless connectivity is ubiquitous. Also, consider a snack area with an accessible beverage center, mail station where portable electronics can be charged, or a seating area that may be a separate but open room with a change in height to define each. Easy access to the outdoors can open up a room and make it seem larger when weather's good.

**Top:** Even when small, a kitchen can function in multiple ways, as designer Joe Human of Designs by Human did in reconfiguring this layout. He opened the living and dining rooms to each other and to the kitchen. There's a tight triangle arrangement for preparations and a comfy counter for eating. **Opposite:** In a striking black and white kitchen, Katherine Shenaman of Katherine Shenaman Interiors designed a big island to accommodate every chef's personal work need, while still being inviting for sitting and eating.

## Caveat

The non-cooking and clean-up stations should ideally be away from cooking spills, heat, and splashing water. Fortunately, because of better technology in products today, there's usually no longer much heat around ranges and ovens. If room in the kitchen allows, designer Jennifer Gilmer likes to have a separate island for clean-up, which is close to the dining room or has a breakfast bar attached to it. If the space doesn't permit for this kind of luxury, putting a prep sink between the refrigerator about 24 to 36 inches (61 to 91 centimeters) from the cooking surface keeps either in an L- or U-shape or in a straight line that keeps cooking contained along this counter area. Then, the clean-up sink can be on the main island, again near the dining areas.

Because today's kitchen is used for more than just preparing meals and cleaning up, choose materials that dazzle and withstand hard wear and tear. Take into account that these multitasking magicians require a good dose of visual balance. Too much cabinetry, while functional, can make a room look claustrophobic and small, so keep some shelves open or floating, don't run them always to the top of the ceiling, and don't use only dark heavy woods or too much reflective surface. The same goes for expanses of flooring and yards of countertops; break them up perhaps with an area rug or different color or pattern, or different backsplash. Add in enough lighting, and different kinds, to perform all desired tasks, and keep the room light by day and night; lighting technology today even allows you to illuminate areas at different levels

and in different colors. Dimmers allow you to vary illumination in one area too—softer, even romantic—over the table, brighter by the range. Think about wiring the room if you love music.

In one kitchen Gilmer designed in a Colonial-style house (above and left), she changed the finish on the wood for the island, added in a harlequin-shaped tile backsplash, and painted some of the walls an aged ochre color. She unified the space with big dollops of white in perimeter cabinets, white on the ceiling, and a travertine tile floor installed on the diagonal.

If your kitchen can accommodate all the activities above, it will truly be the hub of your home. Other rooms in the house become almost superfluous!

**Opposite:** Breaking up cabinetry with open shelves above the microwave and flanking them with glass doors keeps this wall light looking in this Gilmer-designed kitchen. Dark wood base cabinets on the island are finished with turned furniture-style legs. **Top left:** In this multitasking kitchen by Gilmer, a second island separates a kitchen and family room, which houses a wine refrigerator and wall oven. **Top center:** A custom range hood surround breaks up wall cabinets on the range wall. **Top right:** A walnut countertop on the island that separates the family room is illuminated by a pendant that matches the pair over the sink island.

# DINING DIVAS

**CHALLENGE:** Fit in an eat-in option in your kitchen based on the room's size, proportion, and number of diners

A warm, inviting eat-in kitchen provides double duty for today's modern family. But fitting it in requires a carefully thought-out layout, particularly in small galley-size designs. You may also want to orient the dining area to keep sight lines open to a cook, view the outdoors, or watch TV. There are numerous options, from an island to a peninsula, banquette, or traditional table.

An island or peninsula, even short ones, can serve as attractive, practical food prep and eating zones, while isolating this function from the main work areas. But your kitchen has to be large enough to accommodate either of these features. You need at least 39 to 48 inches (1 to 1.22 meters) all

around for traffic to circulate comfortably. If you don't have that much space, consider a very short, narrow island or peninsula that widens or becomes a circle at one end to fit at least two stools or chairs, or a countertop extension that flips up when needed and down when not used. Make the area 42 inches (1.07 meters) high for bar stools, 36 inches (90 centimeters) high for counter stools, or 30 inches (76 centimeters) high for chairs. Be aware that bar stools are harder for young and elderly family members to navigate, although counter-height stools can serve both very well. Any seating on casters means it can be pushed away when not needed.

**Top:** In this kitchen designed by Jennifer Gilmer of Jennifer Gilmer Kitchen and Bath, lightweight stools take up little visual space but invite family members and friends to keep the cook company or serve as sous chef. **Opposite:** Stainless steel cabinets are juxtaposed with glossy white and Wenge cabinetry and shelves to create this cohesive kitchen, breakfast room, and family room combination. Open shelves keep the space light, and a glass backsplash of small subway tile in shades of brown reflects light from the windows and patio doors.

In one kitchen, designer Jennifer Gilmer, along with interior designer Jodi Macklin, designed in a transitional/contemporary mode, a 4-inch (10 centimenters) thick counter that was able to fit both casual peninsula and regular seating. The peninsula only juts out 39 inches (1 meter) but can accommodate two stools; the top is a practical surface for any meal. The round table near a large window is 60 inches (1.52 meters) in diameter, and can easily accommodate six chairs. It's critical to remember that you will want a table centered on a window if one is in the room, both for aesthetics and balance, as well as placement of a chandelier or pendant. The table location will dictate where the light is hung and that light needs to be on center or the room will look poorly designed. "When laying out the space, I often place the table first in a situation like this and then back into the kitchen using the table as a guide for the parameters of the rest of the layout," says Gilmer.

In this kitchen, there are 42 inches (1.07 meters) from the peninsula counter to the round table, which is definitely a minimum when there is going to be both a chair and a counter stool sliding backwards as people finish eating. The client wanted a pendant light above the peninsula to provide illumination for prepping, reading and mood lighting. It was very close to the chandelier above the table, so it was imperative to choose a pendant that would not conflict but rather blend with the more prominent light fixture. Put all lights on dimmers when possible, so that they can be adjusted for the proper task or mood.

**Top:** Gilmer designed a countertop perpendicular off the sink wall to make room for two stools and additional workspace. Careful positioning of light fixtures, a pendant above the dining peninsula, and a chandelier centered above the breakfast table help define both spaces. **Opposite:** Repeating floating Wenge shelves on the kitchen sink wall and in the family room unify the spaces. Gilmer also extends the countertop into the family room to provide space for another base cabinet and wine cooler.

In a warm, wood modern kitchen, Gilmer took a very different approach because a big 10-foot-by-3-foot-6-inch (3 meters by 1 meter) island at the center would serve multiple purposes—eating, prepping, watching a cook prepare, or just having a place to spread out the paper, do homework, pay bills, or snack. The island was topped in a light colored granite called Wasabi, which works well with the mix of birch wood cabinets on perimeters. The very pale yellow painted cabinets form the island, and complement the stacked slate stone behind the range. On all four sides, there's almost 42 inches (1.07 meters) for good circulation to reach equipment and enter and exit the room.

The original kitchen provided the challenge. It would not accommodate a good-sized island like this and the client didn't think it would be possible to make a larger island. They had an oversized walk-in pantry, which housed the metal duct for the downstairs fireplace's flue. By relocating the flue and scaling back the pantry, the clients were able to have their dream island, which is now much more in proportion with the other rooms in their house. "Don't ever feel like what you see and what you have existing in your home is the way that it has to be. Sometimes, changes to the floor plan and moving something as simple as a metal duct can make a world of difference!" explains Gilmer.

**Opposite:** By centering the island on the range, Gilmer draws the eye into the space to glimpse the custom-made hood and stone tile backsplash. Tweaking the existing floor plan slightly allows for a spacious island and a new bank of windows across the back of the house.

Banquettes, associated with 1950s diners, have made a comeback both for nostalgia and because they are highly useful when space is limited. They can also provide useful storage underneath the seating for books and toys or extra kitchen equipment not often used. Upholster the seat and slant the back for comfort. Tuck the banquette into a corner to maximize what often becomes wasted space.

For the smallest kitchens, consider a table that pulls out from a wall like a drawer and slides back into its slot when not in use. Any round table should be at least 36 inches (91 centimeters) in diameter for two; a rectangular shape would be the same, and either could fit four diners in a pinch. A peninsula should have a minimum of 48 inches (1.22 meters) clearance for two but 54 inches (1.37 meters) is better. For one person at a peninsula, 24 inches (61 centimeters) is the minimum width but 30 inches (76 centimeters) is more comfortable.

**Opposite:** Banquettes conserve space and create cozy eating, and for this reason designer Claudia Juestel of Adeeni Design Group takes that route for a one-bedroom rental, where her client formerly had just a rolling island and no place to sit. The custom-designed table has a laminate top and aluminum base and was fabricated by a restaurant manufacturer. **Above:** In the same kitchen, designer Claudia Juestel opens the workspace to the dining area. Paint-grade cabinets, rather than wood, keep the cost down but still add a rich, warm feeling to the room with their ochre hue repeated in the banquette area.

For larger kitchens, you have more options—from round to circular and oval-shaped tables that can even be used for meals with guests, not just family. Think about surfaces that wear well—laminates, quartzes, and woods, for example. Pick seating that complements the table and room's style.

Gilmer and designer Marc Janecki used the length of a kitchen to fit in a comfortable 48-inch (1.22 meters) wood table with seating for four in front of a large flat-screen TV, with a narrow stacked stone tile pattern on the wall; the adjacent wall was used to display some of the homeowners' art collection, proving that a kitchen used daily is a great place to display favorite possessions (above). By arranging equipment and cabinetry carefully, Gilmer also had room for a highly functional island that is dressed up with a Caesarstone top, dentil mold detailing, and oak-stained cabinetry.

Whatever design option you choose, it all boils down to your family's lifestyle, what your kitchen can accommodate in terms of size and proportion, and what you will most enjoy.

**Top:** With ample dining and relaxing space just off the kitchen, designers Jennifer Gilmer and Marc Janecki knew that no seating was needed at the island. Instead, this island houses a beverage cooler and ample storage to conceal cookbooks and other visual clutter.
**Opposite:** Designer Aparna Vijayan of Ulrich Inc. designed a new addition that opens to an adjacent family room and the outdoors, giving the homeowners multiple places to sit and dine. There is a concrete rounded top, a counter with seating, and a more traditional dining table, almost al fresco. A low counter with a sink and beverage center makes entertaining a breeze.

# EXTRA-EXTRA: AUXILIARY ROOMS

**CHALLENGE:** Adding key auxiliary spaces within and beyond a kitchen

These are a home's pragmatic spaces. In the past, the mud room, laundry, and butler's pantry got a rigorous daily workout, yet we often took them for granted. Placed close to a kitchen, garage, or dining room, they were utilitarian rather than aesthetic places to decorate and show off, but no longer! Today, they're high on many wish lists and in the process have grown larger, become a prized feature that can keep traffic out of a kitchen or dining room, and organize increasingly busy lives. Some also take on additional functions as a place to pot plants, wrap presents and stash sports gear.

## Laundry Rooms

No longer stuck away in a basement or garage, laundry rooms are designed to be practical but also look pretty and cheerful, as an important adjunct to enhance family life. Though some equipment can be tucked into a kitchen corner behind doors or pull-down shutters that complement or duplicate kitchen cabinets, laundry machines and supplies are more often placed in a separate room to avoid noise and traffic jams in the kitchen. In their own space, they're often left exposed, though you may still prefer to enclose them behind folding doors. What else makes a laundry well designed and attractive?

- A counter above the washer and dryer is useful if they are side-by-side or, if your machines are stacked, due to space limitations, or have a counter nearby. The counter is a good place to fold freshly washed and dried clothing, and can morph into a place for wrapping presents.

- If there's enough wall space, a built-in ironing board is a great addition—it can be hidden within a closet or be attached to the wall and folded down when you need it.

**Top:** Cubby holes, a bench, and hooks make for great organizing. **Opposite:** A variety of storage types keeps a laundry-cum-mud room tidy and appealing. Desings: Wellborn Cabinet Inc.

- Cabinetry or open shelves can be used to stash laundry detergent, a hamper to transport clothing to bedrooms, hangers, and an iron.

- A full door or pocket door for privacy to the adjacent kitchen.

- A small sink used to rinse out delicate items or soak clothing that's taken a beating.

- Flooring that can stand up to detergent and water spillage. Smart choices are sheet or solid vinyl, ceramic tile, commercially rated Marmoleum (modern day linoleum), or cork.

- A chair or bench added as a spot to sit while waiting for a load to finish.

- Recessed lighting installed to bring the room to life and, if space is limited, painting it a light, bright color. At the same time, don't hesitate to get bold and use color here.

In one kitchen, a butler's pantry was transformed into a kitchen-cum-laundry room designed by decorator Leslie Markman-Stern. Because the same cabinets were used throughout—anigre and cherry— it's impossible to distinguish the zones, with the kitchen to the left and the laundry to the right. The countertops where laundry can be folded is granite. Three different recessed lights above offer general, task, and accent lighting for different functions.

**Top:** Designer Leslie Markman-Stern put the laundry right in the kitchen, using the same cabinets. **Bottom:** Bilotta Kitchens' Randy O'Kane, CKD and senior designer, made a laundry room bright with windows and paint. **Opposite:** The stainless steel refrigerator defines the end of the kitchen and the beginning of the laundry in this space designed by Jennifer Gilmer. Adding cherry panels to the washer and dryer fronts and continuing the countertop makes them almost disappear.

The laundry equipment was originally in this kitchen, but it was closed off with doors and unsightly homemade shelving. Designer Jennifer Gilmer suggested removing the wall to gain space, cleaned up the area by installing smaller-sized units that would fit under the countertop, and used cherry cabinets that match the kitchen. She topped the units with countertops of the same Jerusalem stone. With the wall and doors removed, the entire space is more cohesive and the kitchen appears much larger.

## Mud Rooms

Especially in North America, these have become the new front door. This is where most homeowners enter and exit, and it's typically off or near a garage. If you have extra space, here are some tips on how to make it extra appealing.

- Add a coat closet or rack, a bench with storage underneath and a place to sit to put on sneakers before you head out for a run or game of tennis, and a built-in heater to warm the room and offer a spot to hang items to dry.

- Add cubbies for each family member to individually store their coats, hat, gloves, boots, sports equipment, and backpacks to keep everyone organized.

- If your budget allows, consider installing under-floor heating. Use the same flooring types as you would use in the laundry, rather than wood, which can buckle if the area gets wet.

- If there's even more room, add a large whiteboard, blackboard, or tack board for messages and schedules.

- Make it double as an indoor "garden center" with a sink to pot plants and wash off veggies and fruit from your garden.

In one laundry room, designer Jane Ellison changed the space located right off the kitchen to be practical with slate flooring, durable olive-green cabinetry, and the same marble countertops as in the kitchen. Open shelves were placed by the sink; closed cabinets for cleaning supplies by the equipment. Despite its hard working functions, the room offers an old-fashioned fun feeling. "It had to be a room that was fun to be in, updated from your grandmother's or parents' basement spaces," says Ellison.

## Butler's Pantry

The butler's pantry is making a comeback. Think Downton Abbey for inspiration. Typically located in a hall between the kitchen and dining room, it's packed with conveniences often found in a kitchen, including:

- A small prep sink to wash glasses and silver;

- Extra small appliances to make meal service easier than constantly going back to the kitchen; good helpers include a warming drawer, microwave, small wine cooler, or beverage center;

- Additional storage for more formal dishes and glasses used in the dining room.

If you want to integrate the space into your kitchen or dining room, choose cabinetry, materials, colors, and lighting that coordinate, or get bold and go in a totally different direction for fun.

Good design can make the labor that takes place in these rooms much more pleasurable, based on personal taste, budget, and lifestyle.

**Opposite top left:** Everything has its place—scarves on hooks and shoes in cubbyholes, and there's even a mirror to check hair and make-up; cabinetry from Wellborn Inc. **Opposite top center:** Butler pantries help keep secondary kitchen tasks away from the main work zone, cabinetry from Wellborn. **Opposite top right:** Sleek cabinetry provides accessible storage with wide drawers beneath the countertop in this butler's pantry designed by Paul Bentham of Jennifer Gilmer Kitchen and Bath. **Opposite bottom:** Matching storage columns and benches create organized symmetry, cabinetry from Wellborn Inc.

# OUTDOORS GALORE

**CHALLENGE:** Designing an outdoor kitchen that connects you to nature and allows you to entertain friends and feed the family

Utilizing every square foot of your residence, indoors and out to take advantage of its special qualities is one of the biggest trends in residential construction in recent years. Depending on your domicile, whether a single family home surrounded by a large yard or a high-rise apartment in a chic urban center, this can entail enhancing curb appeal, planting flowers or vegetables in pots on a sky-high balcony, or adding amenities down on the ground in the form of a backyard terrace or deck, a swimming pool or other water feature, a vegetable garden, or a place to cook and eat.

The reasons are simple—living outdoors feels good, is healthy, expands interiors—sometimes exponentially, makes better use of a home's special setting, and takes advantage of Mother Nature's expansiveness.

Depending on your climate, your home's location, size of your yard or decks or balconies, and your particular interests, there are a multitude of ways to create a warm and inviting outdoor space.

**Top:** Lined with fire brick and with a custom grate, this fire pit designed by landscape architect Robert Hursthouse of Hursthouse Landscape Architects and Contractors has a gas starter for easy use. **Opposite:** Designer Jason Urrutia of Urrutia Design, used two sections of doors that open 44 feet (13 meters) to merge the kitchen and dining room with the ipe wood deck.

The easiest plan is to connect your kitchen to the outdoors or to an outdoor-oriented space with large windows or doors—sometimes the entire length of a wall—which can be folded away or raised or lowered easily with the push of a button.

**Left and top:** To extend a kitchen to the outdoors and have room to cook and dine, architect Mark R. LePage of Fivecat Studio Architecture designed a two-level solution to a steep grade. On the upper level, he placed a barbecue and table; down the wide steps and nestled into a stone wall, he fashioned a living space with room for comfortable seating.

Because of the trend to maximize our enjoyment of the outdoors, manufacturers have introduced cooking equipment that's much more elaborate than just a simple barbecue grill—there is an outdoor (weatherproof) version for every type of indoor kitchen appliance. For homeowners who revel in outdoor cooking and entertaining, an outdoor kitchen can rival that of one indoors—with grill, rotisserie, sink, beer tap, pizza oven, icemakers, and mini refrigerators along with storage for cooking utensils, plates, glasses, cutlery, and more. The key is to purchase equipment that's frost-resistant for colder climates, as well as countertops and storage systems that are made to be left outdoors.

Ideally, a well-planned outdoor kitchen should have easy access to the house otherwise long treks will mean you're less likely to use it. Purchase non-breakable but attractive and colorful dishes, glasses, and cutlery that can also be left outdoors. Other parts of your outdoor kitchen should be made of materials that can withstand weather, such as stainless steel for equipment, stainless or teak for storage, and concrete, slate, quartz, or granite for countertops. And remember to install plenty of electrical outlets that meet local safety regulations.

**Top:** This outdoor kitchen, designed by landscape architect Robert Hursthouse, uses a pergola to mimic the material and design of the home. **Opposite top:** Conceived and built by Del Webb, this outdoor patio off the back of a house has been designed for entertaining with a sheltered cooking and serving area. **Opposite bottom:** Designed by Morgante-Wilson Architects, an enticing screened-in porch provides additional space for entertaining, barbecuing, or a quiet place to savor views of Lake Michigan.

It's a good idea to have furniture made of weatherproof materials, such as wrought iron or teak or all-weather wicker. Upholstery and pillows should be made with all-weather fabrics that are able to withstand rain, hot sun, and other challenging weather in case you don't have a place to store them come winter. Consider an umbrella, retractable shade, or pergola to shade hot sun, Don't forget to wire your outdoor area for sound, or at least have an iPod or docking station you can bring outside.

**Opposite:** Landscape architect Jim Bertrand of Bertrand Landscape, started with an old creaky deck facing a golf course, but transformed it into a functional yet comfortable outdoor entertainment area with a kitchen, bar, eating area, intimate sitting area by a fireplace under a pergola, and million-dollar views. **Above left:** Have a table and chairs that can withstand rain and other bad weather when you set up an outdoor dining space. Designer Kristin Okeley of Kitchens by Design also installed a pergola overhead to block sun. **Above right:** Multiple outdoor living "rooms" are connected by the glow of a double-sided fireplace, reflection of falling water, local quarried stone, and soft plantings full of fragrance and color, all selected by landscape designer Laurie Van Zandt from The Ardent Gardener Landscape Design and Project Coordination. Stone work was done by Brion Taylor of BT Stone Masonry.

Fire pits or fireplaces provide a way to stay warm even on the coldest days of winter. Fire pits can be built in or be lightweight and portable. Generally, they are small, about 4 to 6 feet (1.2 to 1.8 meters) in diameter, and 18 to 30 inches high (46 to 76 centimeters), and can use wood logs or gas. Both pits and permanent fireplaces, which are much larger and more expensive, can be constructed from concrete, stone, gravel, brick, slate, or a fire-resistant composite. There are also all sorts of small fire-oriented products, for cooking and entertaining, such as fire bowls that usually include a pourable gel fuel, fire tables that may incorporate a place to ignite a propane gas flame, and wood burning or gas fired ovens that can be used to make more than pizza.

Whatever you choose, in order to get maximum night-time enjoyment, install outdoor lighting in a variety of fixtures, preferably with energy-efficient LEDs, which provide enough illumination for amenities and landscaping, but not so much as to resemble an airport runway or shopping center. Yellow light bulbs and citronella candles keep bugs at bay during the summer. Be sure to include lots of direct light for the prep and cooking area.

Much like the way you designed your indoor kitchen, use space wisely—and that doesn't mean having to adopt the traditional work triangle. Rather, think about how you'll maneuver about the space. Consider the location of other outdoor features such as pools, gardens, trees, fences, and neighbors' houses to maximize privacy. Leave room for traffic to flow throughout, always positioning comfortable seating areas for people to socialize away from the heat, smoke, and cooking aromas of the grill. Then enjoy. This is outdoor living and entertaining at its most sublime, and a true extension of your home.

**Top:** An outdoor kitchen designed by landscape designer Michael Glassman has all the amenities with barbecue, refrigerator, warming draw, burners, stereo speakers, TV, and under-counter lighting under a covered loggia with heaters, fans, lighting, and travertine countertops.
**Opposite:** Landscape designer Michael Glassman built a protected gas fireplace and faced in natural stone in this dining area to provide warmth and ambience on cooler evenings.

# Resources

These resources will help you do a better job of planning
and executing your kitchen design or remodel

## Books

Some of the titles listed below may no longer be
published however, they should still be available at
libraries or through online resources such as Amazon.

Ballinger, Barbara and Glassman, Michael, *The Garden
Bible: Designing your perfect outdoor space*, 2016, The
Images Publishing Group

Buchholz, Barbara B. and Margaret Crane, *Successful
Homebuilding and Remodeling*, 1998, Kaplan Publishing

Casson Madden, Chris, *Kitchens: Information and
inspiration for Making Kitchens the Heart of the Home*,
1993, Clarkson Potter

Country Living, *Country Living 500 Kitchens: Style, Comfort
& Charm*, 2008, Hearst Publishing

Crafti, Stephen, *21st Century Kitchens*, 2010, The Images
Publishing Group

Cregan, Lisa, *House Beautiful Kitchens: Creating a Beautiful
Kitchen of Your Own*, 2012, Hearst Publishing

Cusato, Marianne, *Just Right Home*, 2013, Workman Publishing

Daley, Susan and Steve Gross, *Farmhouse Revival*, 2013,
Abrams

De Giulio, Mick, *Kitchen Centric*, 2010, Balcony Press

Dickinson, Duo, *Staying Put: Remodel Your House to Get
the Home You Want*, 2011, The Taunton Press

Gold, Jamie, *New Kitchen Ideas that Work*, 2012,
The Taunton Press

Hall, Andrew, *100 Great Kitchens and Bathrooms by
Architects*, 2008, The Images Publishing Group

Krasner, Deborah, *The New Outdoor Kitchen: Cooking
up a Kitchen for the Way you Work and Play*, 2009,
The Taunton Press

Means, R.S. and Lexicon Consulting, *Universal Design Ideas
for Style, Comfort & Safety*, 2007, R.S. Means

Powell, Jane and Linda Svendsen, *Bungalow Kitchen*, 2011,
Gibbs Smith

Whitacre, Ellen and Colleen Mahoney, *Great Kitchens:
Designs from America's Top Chefs*, 2001, The Taunton Press

## Websites

**American Council for an Energy-Efficient Economy**
www.aceee.org/consumer

**Building Green**
www.buildinggreen.com

**Building Science**
www.buildingscience.com

**EnergyStar**
www.energystar.gov/

**Forest Stewardship Council**
us.fsc.org

**Green Building Advisor**
www.greenbuildingadvisor.com

**Green Depot**
www.greendepot.com

**Green Seal**
www.greenseal.org

**Guide to Recycling Appliances**
www.partselect.com/JustForFun/Guide-to-Recycling-
Appliances-and-Electronics.aspx

**The American Academy of Healthcare
Interior Designers**
www.asid.org

**The American Institute of Architects**
www.aia.org

**The American Society of Landscape Architects**
www.asla.org

**The Association of Professional Landscape Designers**
www.apld.org

**The Center for Universal Design**
www.ncsu.edu/ncsu/design

**The National Association of Home Builders**
www.nahb.org

**The National Association of the Remodeling Industry**
www.nari.org

**The National Kitchen and Bath Association**
www.nkba.org

**Your Home—Commonwealth of Australia**
www.yourhome.gov.au

## Apps

The choices here are endless and constantly changing.
As of 2013, some good apps include:

**Construction Buddy**
Available on both iPhone and Android devices, this app
offers 35 timesaving tools including wallpaper, concrete,
base trim, carpet, and heating calculators.

**iHandy Carpenter**
This is a virtual workshop that offers tools of the trade.
Great graphics, measuring tools, and more to help you
with your kitchen project.

**Mark on Call**
This app gives you access to a virtual professional and
you can view virtual rooms.

**Photo Measures**
This enables you to take photos of kitchen spaces and
then it calculates the measurements. It also helps you
organize different designs.

**ColorChange**
Allowing you to change the color of your kitchen project until
you find the colors that resonate, this can be an alternative
to paint chips, although bear in mind that the available light in
your kitchen may affect how the color looks.

## Featured Designers and Architects

A.S.D. INTERIORS
www.asdinteriors.com

A.W. Stavish Designs
www.awstavishdesigns.com

Adeeni Design Group
www.adeenidesigngroup.com

Amazing Spaces LLC
www.amazingspacesllc.om

Amy Alper Architects
www.alperarchitect.com

Arch-Interiors Design Group
www.archinteriors.com

Barnes Vanze Architects Inc.
www.barnesvanze.com

Beechwood Landscape Architecture and Construction LLC
www.beechwoodlandscape.com

Bertrand Landscape Design
www.bertrandlandscape.com

Better Kitchens, Inc.
www.betterkitchens.com

Bilotta Kitchens
www.bilotta.com

brooksBerry & Associates
www.brooksberry.com

Cabinets & Design
www.cabinetsdesignslex.com

CG&S Design Build
www.cgsdb.com

Decorating Den
www.GulfCoast.DecoratingDen.com

Decorating Den Interiors
www.sandykozar.decoratingden.com

Decorating Den Interiors
www.decdens.com/lmccall

Decorating Den Interiors Inc.
www.decoratingden.com

Denise Fogarty Interior
www.denisefogarty.com

Design by Human
www.whatisdbh.biz

Designs for Living
www.designsforlivingvt.com

Diane Bishop Interiors
www.dianebishopinteriors.com

Divine Kitchens
www.divinekitchens.com

Drury Design
www.drurydesigns.com

Eisner Design LLC
www.eisnerdesign.com

EMI Interior Design Inc.
www.emiinteriordesign.com

Errez Design
www.errezdesign.com

EvoDOMUS LLC
www.evodomus.com

Feinmann, Inc.
www.feinmann.com

Feldman Architecture
www.feldmanarchitecture.com

Fivecat Studio Architecture
www.fivecat.com

Fredman Design Group
www.fredmandesigngroup.com

Gardner Mohr Architects LLC
www.gardnermohr.com

Garrison Hullinger Interior Design
www.garrisonhullinger.com

Häfele America Co.
www.hafele.com

Hamilton Snowber Architects
chris@hamiltonsnowber.com

Harpole Architects, P.C.
www.jerryharpole.com

Helen Sullivan Design
sullivandesign@aol.com

Hursthouse Design
www.hursthouse.com

In Detail Interiors
www.indetailinteriors.com

Jackson Design and Remodeling
www.jacksondesignandremodeling.com

Jane Ellison Interior Design
www.janeellison.com

Jennifer Gilmer Kitchen and Bath Ltd.
www.jennifergilmerkitchens.com

Jodi Macklin Interior Design
www.jodimacklin.com

Katherine Shenaman Interiors
www.katherineshenaman.com

Kitchen+Bath Design+Construction
www.kb-dc.com

Kitchens by Design
www.kitchensbydesign.net

Leslie M. Stern Design Ltd.
www.lesliemsterndesign.com

Lisa Lougee Interiors
Lisalougee@yahoo.com

Lisa Wolfe Design Ltd.
www.wolfedesign.com

Live-Work-Play
www.live-work-play.net

Lori Carroll and Associates
www.loricarroll.com

Louis Tenenbaum
www.louistenenbaum.com

Marc Janecki Design
www.marcjaneckidesign.com

Michael Glassman and Associates
www.michaelglassman.com

Michelle Workman Interiors
www.michelleworkman.com

Modiani Kitchens
www.modianikitchens.com

Morgante-Wilson Architects
www.morgantewilson.com

Mother Hubbard's Custom Cabinetry
www.mhcustom.com

Neil Kelly Company
www.neilkelly.com

nuHaus
www.nuhaus.com

Orren Pickell Building Group
www.pickellbuilders.com

Pagliaro Bartels Sajda Architects
www.pbs-archs.com

Papyrus Home Design
www.papyrushomedesign.com

Perfect Palette
Mc3409@gmail.com

PulteGroup/Del Webb
www.delwebb.com
www.pultegroup.com

Randall Mars Architects
www.randallmarsarchitects.com

Rossington Architecture
www.rossingtonarchitecture.com

Sarah Barnard Design
www.sarahbarnarddesign.com

SCW Interiors
www.scwinteriors.com

Stephanie Wohlner Design
www.swohlnerdesign.com

Stuart Cohen and Julie Hacker Architects
www.cohen-hacker.com

Susan Agger
agger3909@ad.com

Susan Dowling Interior Design
www.susandowlinginteriors.com

The Ardent Gardener Landscape Design and Project Coordinator
www.theardentgardener.net

The Kitchen Source
www.thekitchensource.net

Thermador
www.thermador.com

Thomas Sarti Girot Interiors
TSGirotinteriors@aol.com

Ulrich Inc.
www.ulrichinc.com

Urrutia Design
www.urrutiadesign.com

Vivian Braunohler
www.braunohlerdesign.com

Wellborn Cabinet Inc.
www.wellborn.com

Your Color Source Studios, Inc. and Color911
www.amywax.com
www.Color911.com

## Appliances

Bosch
www.bosch-home.com

Fisher Paykel
www.fisherpaykel.com

LG Electronics
www.lg.com

Maytag
www.maytag.com

Miele
www.miele.com.au
www.miele.co.uk
www.miele.com

SubZero Wolf
www.subzero-wolf.com

Whirlpool
www.whirlpool.com

# Acknowledgments

Barbara Ballinger | Margaret Crane | Jennifer Gilmer

Well-functioning kitchens are high on most homeowners' wish lists, and they certainly have always ranked high on ours. Each of us has remodeled kitchens for our families multiple times. We are always seeking to fashion a place to spend time socializing with family and friends while being able to work easily. We all enjoy cooking and entertaining, and successful remodeling projects often produce the wonderful side effect of enhancing our homes' property values.

This book is the culmination of all the decades of trial and error that it has taken us to know what to do, and, maybe more importantly, what not to do. Jennifer Gilmer is a kitchen design professional at the top of her game with more than 30-plus years' experience in the trade and 19 years of owning her own firm, based in the Washington D.C. area. Continuing and constant advances in appliances, manufacturing, materials, and lighting keep Jennifer on her toes. She's always learning, researching, and understanding what's out there, which enables her to explain what's what to potential clients—and to us. And we, in turn, do the same for readers of our many articles and web content. We also want to thank Jennifer's two right hands at her firm, Patrice Casey and Priya Gupta, without whom this book could not have been completed.

We also want to thank kitchen designer Jason Landau of Amazing Spaces LLC in Briarcliff Manor, New York, who shared kitchens as well as his expertise, which appears throughout the book in the form of Warnings and Lessons. And thanks also to CoCo Harper of Jackson Remodeling and Design in San Diego, California, who always came through at the 11th hour with another great kitchen when we needed a project to illustrate a particular point.

Many friends, partners, and professionals have helped the three of us through the years, as well as for this big undertaking. We wanted to write a book that would showcase great kitchens visually and in text, but also make the journey from dream to reality as painless as possible. With this book as a guide, kitchen renovation does not have to be the nightmare some describe it to be or have experienced. Those who've helped us most are all the kitchen designers and architects whose projects are showcased within, as well as the homeowners who allowed us to share their redone kitchens.

We are also fortunate enough to be working with one of the finest international publishers of beautiful and information-filled books, The Images Publishing Group. We are especially grateful to Paul Latham and Alessina Brooks for believing in our concept from the get-go and to our editor, Mandy Herbet, for bringing her skills, insight, editing, and passionate dedication to the project. We are also indebted to the rest of the IMAGES family, especially Ryan Marshall and Rod Gilbert for their graphic design expertise.

We are, of course, deeply grateful to our family members and friends who listened to us as we talked ad nauseum about yet another fancy kitchen feature or cool new trend—induction cooktops, separate refrigerator and freezer columns and drawers, porcelain tiles that resemble wood planking, charging stations, family-friendly hubs, and multitasking kitchens for cooking, socializing, gathering, paying bills, and more. And we all dream of how we would like to incorporate our discoveries in our next kitchen or cooking space—thick white marble countertops, wide reclaimed plank floors, or an outdoor kitchen with a pizza oven in the garden.

We hope you enjoy and benefit from our efforts as much as we have.

# Photography Credits

**Front Cover**
Bob Narod

**Back Cover**
Bob Narod (left)
Olson Photographic (center left)
Courtesy, Adeeni Design Group (center right)
Celia Pearson (right)

**Chapter One**
Bob Narod 11, 12, 14, 17, 18, 21, 22

**Chapter Two**
Bob Narod 27, 28, 33, 34
Lucy Shappell 37
Jennifer Gilmer Kitchen and Bath Ltd.
  floor plans 29, 30, 33

**Chapter Three**
Bob Narod 39, 40, 41, 42, 43, 45 (center),
  46, 47, 48, 51, 52, 53, 54, 55, 56, 57
Celia Pearson 44, 45 (left and right)

**Chapter Four**
James Tetro 59, 60, 62, 63, 65

**Chapter Five**
Hafele America Co. 69, 70, 71
Courtesy, Neil Kelly Company 72

**Chapter Six**
Bob Narod 75, 76, 77, 78 (above left), 79
Thermador 78, (above center, above top
  right, and bottom right), 80, 81
Colby Edwards 83

**Chapter Seven**
Bob Narod 85

**Small and Budget**
Gridley + Graves Photographers 86, 87
Bob Narod 88, 89, 96, 97
David Young-Wolff 90 (left)

Jon Miller/Hedrich Blessing 90 (center)
Todd Pierson 90 (right)
Nick Novelli Photography 91
PreviewFirst Photography 92 (left)
Greg Riegler 92–93
Steven Mays Photography 94, 95

**Long and Sometimes Narrow**
Bob Narod 98, 99, 100, 101, 104, 105 (left),
  106
Linda Oyama Bryan 102
Jay Greene Photography 103
Nick Novelli 105 (right)
Drury Design 107 (left)
Brad Nicol 107 (right)
Loretta Berardinelli 108
Erika Bierman 109

**Workhorses**
Bob Narod 110, 111, 112, 113, 116
Jon Miller/Hedrich Blessing 114
Memories TTL, LLC, for Modiani Kitchens,
  Englewood, NJ 115
Alise O'Brien Photography 117

**Stylemakers**
Bob Narod 118, 119, 120, 121, 122, 123,
  124, 125, 126, 127, 128, 129
Jack Wolford 130
Eric Roth 130–131
Top Kat Photography 131 (above)
Paul Dyer 132
Joseph Lapeyra 133
Celia Pearson 134, 135

**White Winners**
Bob Narod 136, 137, 138, 139, 140, 141, 142
Tom Olcott 143
Tony Valainis Photography 144, 145

**Colorful Creations**
Bob Narod 146, 147, 150, 151, 157 (left)
Brian Bookwalter 148–149
Blackstone Edge Studio 149 (small shot)
Thomas McConnell 152
Sheila Addleman Photography 153
PreviewFirst 154
Olson Photographic 155
Tony Valainis 156
Photography, Courtesy, Adeeni Design
  Group 157 (right)
Peter Rymwid Photography 158–159
Photography by JohnPaul, John Paul Soto
  159 (top right)
Courtesy of Designs for Living 159
  (bottom right)

**Open-Style Kitchens**
Bob Narod 162, 163, 168 (lower),
  170–171
Annie Garner-Let It Shine Photography
  164–165 (left)
Eric Rorer Photography and Jason Madara
  Photography 165 (above)
©Tyler Chartier, www.TylerChartier.com
  166 (top)
John Umberger, Real Images Inc. 166
  (above left and above right)
Kevin Sprague 167 (top left)
Jason Kindig 167 (top right)
Gordon Beall 168 (top)
PreviewFirst 169
Brian Bookwalter 171 (above)

**Family-Friendly Hubs**
Bob Narod 172, 173, 174–175, 175 (top)
Anice Hoachlander 176, 177
Greg Weiner 178
Loretta Benardinelli 179

PreviewFirst 180
Eric Roth 181 (top left and right)
Codis, Inc. 181 (lower)

**Multitasking Magicians**
Bob Narod 182, 183, 185, 185, 192, 193
Dennis Martin 186 (top)
William Lesch 186-187
Edie Ellison 188-190
Annie Garner/Let It Shine Photography 190
Brantley Photography 191

**Dining Divas**
Bob Narod 194, 195, 196, 197, 198–199, 202
Verite 200, 201
Peter Rymwid Photography 203

**Extra-Extra: Auxiliary Rooms**
Wellborn Cabinet Inc. 204, 205, 208 (top
  left, top center, bottom)
Bob Narod 207, 208 (top right)
Paul Schlismann 206 (top)
Peter Rymwid Photography 206 (bottom)

**Outdoors Galore**
Hursthouse Landscape 210, 214
Matt Sartain Photography 211
Scott LePage Photography, Charlotte, NC
  212–213, 213
Courtesy Del Webb 215 (top)
Tony Soluri 215 (bottom)
Linda Oyama Bryan 216
Tony Valainis 217 (left)
Laurie Van Zandt, The Ardent Gardener
  217 (right)
Michael Glassman 218, 219

**Acknowledgments**
Bob Narod 223 (left and right)
Brian Vanden Brink 223 (center)